INSIGHT INTO

ANGER

INSIGHT INTO

ANGER

Chris Ledger and Wendy Bray

Published 2007 by CWR, Waverley Abbey House, Waverley Lane, Farnham, Surrey GU9 8EP, UK. Registered Charity No. 294387. Registered limited company No. 1990308.

Concept development, editing, design and production by CWR

Printed in England by CPD

ISBN: 978-1-85345-437-0

WAVERLEY ABBEY
INSIGHT SERIES

The Waverley Abbey Insight Series has been developed in response to the great need to help people understand and face some key issues that many of us struggle with today. CWR's ministry spans teaching, training and publishing, and this series draws on all of these areas of ministry.

Sourced from material first presented over Insight Days by CWR at their base, Waverley Abbey House, presenters and authors have worked in close co-operation to bring this series together, offering clear insight, teaching and help on a broad range of subjects and issues. Bringing biblical understanding and godly insight, these books are written both for those who help others and those who face these issues themselves.

CONTENTS

FOREWORD

Anger, according to the *Oxford English Dictionary*, is 'extreme or passionate displeasure'. This definition will hardly do as an explanation of the rich and contradictory emotions that make up this confusing and puzzling word. We have all known anger. I have, and you have. None of us has excuses to offer, but there have been times when we have felt that the anger we expressed was not wholly wrong, was not always bad and indeed, may have actually done some good. On the other hand, we can all think of those painful moments in a stressful situation when, instead of biting our tongue or submitting with grace, we have retaliated with violent words or, even worse, violence itself.

The fact is that there are so many questions about anger. When does peevishness, bad temper, irritability and plain grumpiness end, and anger begin? What about the link between anger and violence? We all know the story of Jesus who, in His righteous anger, made a 'whip of cords' and drove the shopkeepers out of the Temple. We are not told if He hurt anybody but what is described is a violent act. This may well approximate to what Shakespeare calls 'noble anger' in *King Lear*. But noble anger, protest and displeasure will not do for King Lear. His anger directed towards his daughters, because of their treatment of him, boiled over into revenge. He wanted blood. Little wonder that *King Lear* is one of Shakespeare's darkest Tragedies as he explores human weakness. That story is far from unusual. We have only to think of road rage as car drivers wave their fists in fury or mouth obscenities at other road users, to note the presence of anger in modern life. When it spills over into violence, as it does more frequently than we would like to admit, we can acknowledge the power of anger in daily life.

In this excellent exploration of anger from a Christian point of view, Chris Ledger and Wendy Bray dig deep into the psychology of anger and what it does to us if we allow it to dominate our emotional lives. They handle it in a balanced and mature way, showing that anger can be a normal, healthy, human emotion, but when it controls us, rather than we controlling it, it has the potential to become a destructive, malevolent force that may destroy personal relationships and affect adversely the quality of our lives. What is particularly attractive about this examination of anger is not only the incisive pastoral suggestions about how we may master it, but also how we may redirect its energy into positive service for ourselves and others.

From time immemorial anger has been one of the Seven Deadly Sins. Chris Ledger and Wendy Bray show how the love of God found in Christ is more than able to conquer its power.

George Carey. 103rd Archbishop of Canterbury
(On his retirement in 2002 George Carey was made a life-peer, as Lord Carey of Clifton)

INTRODUCTION

Mention the word 'anger' to a randomly selected group of ordinary men, women and children and each one will respond differently.

Some will immediately recall a recent outburst of anger which has been directed towards them and from which they are still reeling; others will be aware of their own underlying angry feelings. As discussion progresses each may choose to illustrate their anger in different ways: a clenched fist, a raging bull, a balloon about to burst, a simmering pot.

Our personal view of anger and its place in our lives is unique. It will be dependent on our personality, our life experience and our ability to handle the angry emotions we experience in ourselves and in others.

However we perceive anger – and some of us live in fear of it – it's important to recognise that anger is just one little letter – 'd' – away from 'danger'; consequently we need to be aware of its risks. Those who live with the persistent anger of a partner or family member, boss or neighbour will recognise the risk of living in a place where anger makes mouths – and sadly, sometimes fists – work faster than minds.

This practical book aims to help us understand anger, its roots, causes and development. It offers a biblical perspective on anger, explores how God models anger, and considers how we might express our anger to Him in a healthy way.

It also introduces strategies for dealing with both our own anger and the anger of other people: strategies which, with practice and commitment, can be incorporated into the bank of life and communications skills we draw upon each day. For some of us, those strategies will be life-changing; for a few they may even be life-saving.

Wendy Bray

NOTE FROM CHRISTINE LEDGER

Are you an angry person? No, I would reply . . . after all I don't often lose my temper. Well, that would have been my reply until I undertook counselling training! Then I came to realise that all my teenage moodiness, and all the times I have given others 'the silent treatment' was an expression of anger. Anger is a sign that something is wrong, or out of balance in our life, or in the world. This emotion can take many forms and expressions – from the destructive to the constructive. It is wrong when we let anger boil over and allow it to damage others, or we hold onto it so long that it turns into bitterness. However, anger can be used constructively when we harness it to provide energy and courage to change situations ... we see Jesus doing this.

The contents of this book are from a CWR Insight Day I had the privilege to present. It is for those who experience anger, and for others who help and counsel people struggling with destructive anger. Hopefully the material will give a clear insight into and understanding of this emotion, together with skills to handle anger more constructively. Again Wendy has done a brilliant job in taking my notes from the Insight Day and adding her own unique contribution to create a book which I hope you will find very useful.

CHAPTER 1

WHAT IS ANGER?

INTRODUCTION

Anger is often viewed as a negative emotion – especially by Christians.

It is seen as an emotion to be tamed, battled with – even denied. We are embarrassed by anger, shamed by it, and may do all we can to cover it up or banish it with excuses. In doing so, we are mistaking its purpose and function: for anger is a complex God-given gift that we should not ignore.

WHAT IS ANGER *FOR*?

Anger has many sources – and we'll discuss those later – but it also has many functions. Those of us who have always believed that all anger is wrong may be surprised at the positive nature of those functions: not the things that anger rises up against, but what it is *for*.

Understanding what anger is for may help us to realise that it is not always a negative emotion, but part of a normal, healthy, emotional make-up – usually for a very good reason.

Anger
- draws our attention to hurts and wounds;
- helps us identify fear so that we can protect ourselves if necessary;
- energises us to put wrongs right.

Anger locates hurt by giving a voice to the pain of unmet needs, to a sense of rejection, perhaps, or to emotional or physical hurt that we may have left unvoiced – often for years.

Sometimes we may not even be aware of our hurt until a single incident or word triggers an angry response. Then our anger reveals what we may have been unknowingly hiding: that, for example, we do *very much* mind if our boss takes us for granted, we are left out of a guest list once more or we are expected to put up with unreasonable demands or behaviour from a relative without complaint.

Anger may also seek to protect. When our lives are under threat, an angry response is often the first response, in partnership with fear. If faced with a mugger, most of us would follow our instantaneous shock and surprise with an innate sense of outrage which says, 'I will not let this happen'. We might become angry and perhaps lash out, fighting to protect ourselves.

A parent's anger at their child's recklessness or risk-taking is similar. Many a relieved parent of a teenager has burnt up the joy and relief they have felt at their son or daughter's safe arrival home with explosive fury at the risk they have entertained: 'Where *have* you been?!' They are asking not so much for a description of the nightclub as for a teenage recognition of the place of danger the night itself has become!

The most appropriate and selfless anger energises us to change a situation, or take action to force that necessary change. Bob Geldof's 'Live Aid' – and later 'Live8' – project is a shining example of motivating anger in the face of others' need, as are broader campaigns like 'Make Poverty History' and 'Stop the Traffik': movements motivated by a sense of anger at the injustice towards, and the degradation of, fellow human beings.

The multi-faceted personality that anger shows the world means that a clear and simple definition is problematic. Perhaps the most all-encompassing is that of the *Penguin English Dictionary*,[1] which says that anger is *'a strong feeling of displeasure'*. Others would say that is it an emotional response to pain.

If anger is 'an emotional response to pain', our first step towards understanding it may involve recognising one facet of anger as an outward symptom, or sign, of some kind of inward pain; an expression or feeling which manifests itself in response to pain and hurt, like the rawness and exposure of an open wound.

Invariably there will be two types of wound: a wound which has resulted from hurt and rejection and a wound inflicted by fear, perhaps of loss or change. Both wounds smart with anger.

Our reaction to a thoughtless boss will cause the first type of wound and our furious but relieved parent of a teenager will reel from the pain of the second.

IT'S AN ANGRY WORLD

Despite the positive functions of anger, society's immediate relationship with it is generally a negative one: it's an increasingly angry world out there.

There are 'wars and rumours of wars', most started in anger. Street violence is commonplace – and not just in our largest towns and cities. Anger is even given entertainment status by programme-makers in talk-shows and 'reality' TV; radio debates often jam our airwaves with aggression and argument.

In Britain, a nation historically known for its mild manners and stoical approach to life, one in ten of us admit to losing our temper at least once a day and increasing numbers of personal relationships are destroyed by anger. Medical staff are frequently on the receiving end of anger from patients and their families. One in six NHS staff has been attacked[2] while, on average, two NHS staff will be violently or verbally attacked in Scotland every hour of the day.[3] The Department of Health reported 65,000 recorded incidents of violence to health workers on home visits in a single year.[4]

Domestic violence accounts for 16 per cent of all violent crime.[5] The victims are repeatedly abused more than any other crime (on average there will have been thirty-five assaults before a victim calls the police) and this sort of crime claims the lives of two women each week and thirty men per year. It is the largest cause of morbidity worldwide in women aged nineteen to forty-four, greater than war, cancer or motor vehicle accidents, and will affect one in four women and one in six men in their lifetime.

So called 'road rage', whilst not an official driving offence, is on the increase, especially in cities: 87 per cent of drivers claim that they have been a 'road rage' victim at least once, while 20 per cent say they have experienced it more than ten times.[6]

Anger costs financially, as well as emotionally, jacking up costs for the health service, insurance companies, local councils and police authorities. Widespread, unchecked Internet use exposes adults, young people and children to violent and pornographic images on a regular basis and DVDs portraying violent acts are easily accessible, modelling language, lifestyle and violence which both fuel, and give expression to, anger.

We are an angry people. According to our definition, that inevitably means that we are also a hurting people.

Society in the West is becoming increasingly emotionally dysfunctional, with one third of us suffering from a degree of emotional disturbance – anxiety, depression and anger – that will warrant some form of social, medical or psychiatric intervention.

Two major changes in society – the breakdown of family life and the development of Internet and audio visual technology – arguably contribute to 'the anger effect'. The relationship between those two changes – busy or distant parents relying on computers and TV/DVD for their children's entertainment and the accidental 'education' they offer – is a significant part of that effect. Few families eat together regularly, denying themselves the opportunity to talk, raise and resolve issues in a natural way. Extended families that live close together providing mutual emotional and practical support are increasingly rare. As adults, we are becoming a disconnected society with little time to talk or listen, communicating more by email and text than face to face.

Few of us will be surprised that conversation was officially named by a newspaper[7] as a top twenty skill that is dying out. Minimal communication means that unresolved issues are not raised naturally within supportive relationships. They are suppressed, emerging later as anger.

There is also a personal medical cost. A chronically angry person is twice as likely as a 'laid back' person to have a heart attack and six times more likely to have a heart attack than a smoker or someone with high cholesterol.[8]

We cannot escape anger: it is in the air we breathe. Very few of us will pass through a day without encountering, experiencing or exhibiting anger in some shape or form. Yet many people suppress anger because they feel, or have been taught from an early age, that it is not a good emotion. Unable or unwilling to deal with, or even admit, their anger, they bury it with disastrous consequences.

Even if we do deal with anger on the surface, it can make us lose our perspective and distort our view of the issues – or the person – we are dealing with. When angry, we fail to see either straight or clearly.

Whether we are calm, appear to be calm yet bottle things up, or are prone to angry outbursts, we cannot divorce personality from anger. Acknowledging the link between the two will help us to understand and manage not only our own anger but the anger of others.

IN PRACTICE

EXPRESSING ANGER

Anger may be expressed both actively and passively. Often we don't recognise passive anger, especially if we don't share the personality type of the person standing before us, who, unbeknown to us, is in an angry state.

(When upset, Chris used to be very moody with sullen silences; it was only when undergoing counselling training that she realised this was a passive form of anger.) When we are talking to – or listening to – an angry person, it's important to understand their anger from their viewpoint. The questions we ask must be designed to answer the questions: 'What does this anger mean for you? What is it about? Tell me something about it and put it into other words.'

We may need to help one another express our anger specifically. Not by putting words in one another's mouths, but by helping the right words to be found: 'rage', 'fury', 'explosion', 'fear', 'frustration', 'hate', 'pain', 'insecurity', 'revenge', 'blame', 'stress' 'embittered', etc.

When words are hard to find – with children for example – it may also be helpful to return to the idea of pictures. What shape does your anger take? What colour is it? What is your anger doing? Which animal would your anger be – and why?

Being able to express our anger specifically can be vital in getting right at the roots of our anger and dealing with it at source.

WHAT DO WE BELIEVE ABOUT ANGER?

Like any part of our value system, the beliefs we have about anger are formed from an early age through a myriad of experiences. What we have been taught, and witnessed and experienced of anger will tread pathways of understanding through it. Some of those pathways will be helpful and carry us where we need to go.

Others will be emotional dead ends, fraught with difficulty or littered with snares to trip us up! There, anger *will* spell danger.

When we examine our beliefs about anger, it is helpful to consider whether they are myth or reality and to be prepared to revisit – and often re-route – those pathways.

ANGER: THE MYTHS AND REALITY

Joe Griffin, a psychologist at the European Therapy Studies Institute, and Director of Studies at Mindfields College, researches into effective mind/body communication in clinical and health care settings and has suggested four main myths associated with anger. They are very much up for debate, as personal experience and professional practice – the authors' included – may suggest otherwise. But they do give us a useful starting point for the application of research into anger.

MYTHS

1. 'It is helpful to express anger, eg by beating a pillow.'
   Griffin's research says 'no'.
2. 'It's healthy to let off steam.'
   Studies[9] dispute the efficacy of 'letting off steam' and show that outbursts perpetuate anger and escalate health risks, from heart disease to cancer.
3. 'Talking out your anger will make you less angry.'
   Similarly, research doesn't bear this out.
4. 'Repressed anger causes depression.'
   This is not considered to be the case.[10]

Myth One: 'It is helpful to express anger, eg by beating a pillow.'
The idea that we should always express our anger has a Freudian

origin, respecting the status of this popular 'myth'. Yet research shows that expressing anger in this way is actually destructive. While Freudian theory suggests that we carry around repressed anger that must be discharged in one way or another to avoid neurosis, recent research takes that view to the opposite end of the spectrum.

Over 400 research projects cited by Griffin show that encouraging people to express anger outwardly actually makes that anger worse because it stimulates the fight or flight response and initiates a destructive process.

Chris argues that her work in a professional setting has shown that sometimes helping people express their anger safely can be therapeutic:

> I sometimes work creatively with clients who are finding it difficult to let their anger go. I may use paper and pencil work; I may suggest the client expresses their anger in drawing or painting; or I may work with soft toys. Some of the artwork drawn and painted by clients has been very expressive and very therapeutic. Working with soft toys for some clients can also be a real key in helping them discharge their anger. For example, a soft toy may symbolise the client's abuser and a woman may choose one of my soft toys (invariably an ugly-looking monkey, lion or gorilla) to work with.
>
> I suggest they take it home and express anger towards this symbolic representation of their abuser, in whatever way they wish to. In other words, I support the client in what they choose to do with the soft toy because working things out in their own way will have special meaning for them. In order to discharge the unresolved energy of anger, clients have trodden on them, thrown them round the room, left them out in the garden to freeze to death, and put a paper bag

over the toy's head to suffocate it, with one client putting her soft toy in a plastic bag and tying it up with knots to make sure it was well and truly dead! And it was – for the anger within her consequently also died. For those who find this a helpful way to express and discharge their raw feelings, it moves them on through their unresolved anger and can have a very positive outcome for anger resolution. (Note: not every client will find this approach helpful.)

There *are* important exceptions to such resolution. In extreme cases expressing anger can mean that the anger remains unresolved. Expressing anger, in these cases, merely 'rehearses' the anger, maintaining its expression. It may also lead to suicidal tendencies, where suicide is thought to be the only way to express deep anger to the object of that anger: a family member, spouse or abuser. Consequently, encouraging people to express anger sometimes keeps them in the angry place unable to move on.

Failing to express anger at all can be just as harmful: 'Angry arguments between parents can scar the children – but so can staying icily silent' says Michele Kirsch:[11]

A new study, by the University of Rochester in New York, tells us that it is not only obvious stuff – lobbing frying pans, shouting and swearing – that distresses children but also the more subtle, simmering resentment practised by families who pride themselves on never fighting in front of the children.

Patrick Davies, the psychologist who conducted the research, says, 'With parents who tried to contain anger, or express it as the silent treatment, we found that kids pick up on that just as much as more open hostilities and they expressed anxiety, and a watchful attention, worried about what might happen next.'

The usefulness, or not, of openly expressing anger means that we may need to keep an open mind as we seek to help others with their anger. Some who are stuck in a place of anger may need to choose to move on. Others, who are prepared to move on, may need a safe way to express their anger before doing so.

Myth Two: 'It's healthy to let off steam.'
Whilst research[12] disputes the myth, Chris can see value in a controlled release of anger:

> I actually think it can be healthy to let off steam. I have had a very ill daughter, and in the early years I became very frustrated and angry with the situation. I was powerless, helpless. Fear became anger, because I feared that I could not make her better. So that fear and coming to terms with the fact that I am actually not Superwoman, can't fix everyone, can't fix my daughter, was hard.
>
> I used to cycle to work, and while pedalling away, shout really loud! No one could hear. The traffic would drown it. But it actually got rid of all the pent-up frustration and anger and was very therapeutic for me as I was able to let it go.

Myth Three: 'Talking out your anger will make you less angry.'
When talking 'rehearses' reasons for anger, the angry person continually revisits their emotion, trying to justify why they are angry rather than acknowledging it and moving on.

Very often, when we discuss why we are angry with our spouse, partner or friends – relaying an incident in our day, for example – our conversation becomes little more than a continual sounding out of our reasons for being angry. As a result we often become even angrier and may even find more 'evidence' to support our 'case' as we talk things out, often enlisting the collusion of our companions to do so. It takes a skilled listener to help us dismantle and examine the form and mechanics of our anger rather than allowing us to build upon it.

Myth Four: 'Repressed anger causes depression.'
In an effort to address an escalating problem of widespread depression, the US Government[13] commissioned an investigation of all research studies – over 100,000 – carried out in relation to the illness. Clear guidelines on how depression should be treated were drawn up on the basis of which techniques actually worked in practice. Putting people in touch with their anger was indicated as contrary to helping people with depression to move on.

It is well known, however, that people with depression are often hiding deep anger or loss, and psychological literature often refers to depression as 'anger turned inward'. Depressed people can alternate between feeling angry at themselves and angry at others. Anger and depression can be so closely knit together that it's sometimes hard to know where one ends and the other begins.

When we are hurt as a child, our anger may have been repressed for so long that it is not recognisable as such. It will often manifest itself as illness, phobia, or self-sabotage. We may be unable to experience joy because of deep-seated anger that is literally smothering any positive emotional expression. Often the result is depression.

Childhood is often the place where the seeds of anger are first sown. It is natural for children to feel angry when they are abused or rejected, or when they are constantly put down, because anger comes from feeling hurt, betrayed and abandoned, and from feelings of helplessness and vulnerability. Many children do not have the ability to process these feelings, or are not allowed to, so their feelings of anger can be repressed. The child is not able to admit to him or herself that he or she is angry, so the anger is denied and turned inward. In his book, *The Psychology of Melancholy*, Matthew Ostow writes, 'Depression, at every phrase of its development, includes a component of anger, whether visible or invisible, whether conscious or unconscious.'[14]

This unconscious strategy of burying anger is harmful because the anger doesn't spontaneously dissipate: it remains to do damage psychologically as well as physically.

Denied or unrecognised anger fuels depression, 'which is intensified when there is also a pervasive sense of guilt, for perhaps being angry in the first place'.[15]

It is important to explore our inner world with the courage to face memories from the past that may be recreating anger in the present. Essentially, it is the *power* of our memories that can inflame our anger now. The feelings these memories generate need to be processed and worked through, with counselling or through the ministry of healing.

It's not always quite so simple, of course. To move out of depression, a depressed person needs to be strongly motivated behaviourally. People who are very depressed are often unable even to get out of bed in the morning, so that achievement may need to be the first goal. Consequently they are unable, at first, to examine their anger.

Once behavioural work is made a priority – for example CBT (cognitive behavioural therapy) which sits comfortably with a Christian approach to counselling – we can begin to address issues of anger.

In seeking to help those whose lives are gripped by anger and depression, we need to care for the whole person and that means beginning with their immediate needs.

WHAT DOES THE BIBLE SAY ABOUT ANGER?

Misunderstanding the nature and function of anger from God's perspective, means that some Christians believe that anger is unacceptable. They remain calm on the outside, whilst seething on the inside, failing to see that anger can be healthy, particularly when it is used to bring about positive change.

Many Christians find anger difficult, yet anger is, clearly, biblical. Indeed, we could say that the angriest person in the Bible is God, as we read more about God being angry, than any other 'character'! God's anger is mentioned 455 times in the Old Testament and 375 in the New. It is not surprising, therefore, that Jesus was able to express His anger in a healthy and appropriate way.

Jesus showed that sometimes it is entirely appropriate – indeed, important – to be angry. The real question isn't whether we *should* be angry, but *how* we should be angry: how we express our anger appropriately, deal with it and move on.

As Jesus is our role model for anger management, it is worth examining the context and expression of His anger, as portrayed in the Gospels.

Jesus told Satan to leave in no uncertain terms (Matthew 4:10)
Jesus was in the desert for forty days while Satan was tempting Him. When Satan offered Jesus world domination, Jesus challenged his claims and angrily sent Satan packing, using Scripture to do so, telling him we are to 'Worship the Lord [our]

God, and serve him only'.

Similarly, it's important that we allow ourselves to be outraged when Satan tries to deceive us. We can challenge his claims using Scripture for authority, and our experience of God's faithfulness as evidence.

When we are helping people who have been hurt, we may actually feel a righteous anger in praying for them because of what has happened to them. That anger is an illustration of 'Get behind me, Satan. How dare you ruin this person's life?'

Jesus was angry at injustice (eg Matthew 9:1–8; Luke 13:10–17)
Throughout the Gospels, Jesus was angry with the Jewish leaders because of their self-righteous arrogance and the way in which they put impossible burdens on God's children.

Such anger is justified when we witness ways in which some sections of society, or parts of the world, abuse other parts. For example, the fact that so few of us live in developed countries and yet consume more than half of the world's energy and most of its available fresh water should make us angry! That's righteous anger. It's anger that motivates us to make change happen. In doing so we are acting to 'remove the impossible burdens' still placed on God's children.

Jesus was angry at blasphemy and indifference (Matthew 21:13)
What is possibly Jesus' most well-known angry outburst occurred when He found men in the Temple selling cattle, sheep and doves; and money-changers doing business.

His message was clear and direct: 'Get … out of here! How dare you turn my Father's house into a market!' (John 2:16). He overturned tables in His anger: anger which blazed as much at the abuse of God's free gift of forgiveness as at unethical trading; anger aimed at the similarly overturned values of a just and righteous God.

We can also be justifiably angry when we see those values overturned: angry at the number of abortions recorded each week; the widespread trafficking of people for slavery of so many kinds; the exploitation of God's precious gift of sex; the unfair distribution of the planet's resources; the corruption of big business. Then our anger is not just righteous – but necessary.

But how do we express that anger *God's* way?

The biblical way of handling anger is not to hold onto it, rather to express it – but to do so appropriately. Although righteous anger is acceptable, *personally* induced anger isn't. Paul tells us, '"In your anger do not sin"; Do not let the sun go down while you are still angry, and do not give the devil a foothold' (Eph. 4:26–27). In other words, don't hold onto your anger because if you do it's likely to lead you into sin; express it if it's right, deal with it quickly and appropriately – and move on.

In general terms, anger is not wrong; it is not right. It just *is*. Like the weather, it is a fact of life. On any one day the weather can range from sunshine to downpours – often on the same day! But we wouldn't say either type of weather was *wrong*. One kind may be a little more pleasant or less wet than the other; more damaging or unpredictable, but neither is *wrong*. We just have to respond to that weather appropriately: bikini or umbrella! Similarly, it's how we deal with anger that can be judged right or wrong: how we express it that is appropriate or inappropriate.

Often it is the confusion between feeling anger and dealing with it that ties so many Christians up in knots: 'I shouldn't be angry!'; 'Anger is a sin!' But it's OK to be angry – because anger just *is*. It's how we deal with it that matters.

Anger is such a part of us that there is even a chemical pattern for it – which we'll look at later. That pattern will be present in all of us, because we have all been made in the image of God. God was – is – angry, and so will we be.

Anger that isn't dealt with or which is allowed to continue will inevitably be denied or suppressed; pushed down and stored away for the future. But it doesn't just sit quietly. It busies itself producing resentment that can go on and on – and on.

That's not how God wants us to deal with our anger. He doesn't want us to 'give the devil a foothold' that he can use to enter our lives and do his work.

Jesus, whilst appropriately angry, was also serious about the effects of anger. In fact he likens anger to murder: 'You're familiar with the command to the ancients, "Do not murder." I'm telling you that anyone who is so much as angry with a brother or sister is guilty of murder … The simple moral fact is that words kill' (Matt. 5:21–22, *The Message*).

Strong words indeed: when we are inappropriately or excessively angry we may be guilty of 'murder', because words kill. Murder can't be undone. When we are angry the words that spill out cannot be taken back. The harm cannot be undone. We have hurt someone and damaged their very lives.

Chris tells the story of a six-year-old boy whose birthday was some months ahead:

> As children do, he was already thinking about possible presents. So he asked his mum and dad, 'Could I have a dog for my birthday?' To his delight they agreed: 'Yes you can. Wait until your birthday and you can have a dog.'

During the wait that followed they saw a wonderful wooden kennel in the sales.

So the little boy asked, 'Can I have that for the dog?' His parents agreed that they would buy the kennel and keep it outside for the dog, but that it would remain empty until the dog arrived on the boy's birthday.

Now, this little boy had as many angry outbursts as any six-year-old and his mum and dad decided that they must try to help him to manage his anger healthily. So they said to him, 'Every time you have a really angry outburst we want you to go outside to that kennel and bang a nail into it.'(OK – not such a sensible pursuit for a six-year-old … but it *is* just a story!)

Sometimes he would be out there banging in a nail as much as five times a day! After a while, he had banged about fifty nails into the roof and walls of the kennel. In the process, he got rather bored with his anger and the hammering consequences; so bored, in fact, that he didn't have angry outbursts any more. The problem of uncontrolled anger was solved.

But his clever mum and dad went one step further. They said 'Now that you can check your anger and deal with it well, every day that is free of an angry outburst we want you to go and take one of those nails out of the kennel, so that you can see your progress.' So every day without an angry outburst, the little boy went outside and took a nail out, until all the nails were out. It was a triumph.

But then the little boy looked at the kennel and thought, Look at it. I've messed it up, haven't I? It's full of holes! Supposing my dog goes in there and the rain comes through and it gets wet? It's not a nice cosy home any more. I've ruined it!

He told his parents and they lovingly explained, 'Well, that's the effect of uncontrolled anger. Anger hammers holes in people's lives, it hurts them and leaves scars – like holes – behind.' It was a hard lesson for the little boy to learn – but a vivid one.

THE DIFFERENCES BETWEEN GOD'S ANGER AND HUMAN ANGER

So how does God's anger – righteous anger – compare to human anger?

God's anger is ...	Human anger is ...
Controlled	Out of control
Unselfish	Selfish and self-centred
Without resentment	With resentment and spite
An expression of love	An expression of revenge
To bless relationships	To break relationships
At injustice	At desecration of self
At stubbornness and disobedience	At those who deny me what I want

God's anger is always within His control. Human anger is all too often out of control. God's anger is unselfish and for the good of others. Our own anger, when destructive or inappropriate, is selfish, wanting its own gain. God's anger is without resentment or hate but our anger is often because we resent or hate something or someone. God's anger is an expression of love: it comes out of His desire to do the best for each of us.

God's anger is also against injustice – the best of ours should be too. If we become angry about abortion, poverty or injustice, we may be angry because we are thinking about what is best for those involved; how what is happening to them ignores God's ways. Usually, however, our anger isn't an expression of the 'best', but of the 'worst' – an expression of jealousy, revenge, hate or selfishness. Our anger is often a violation of self. While God's anger is at wilful disobedience, our anger is often against those who cross us.

But we do experience righteous anger when we see an injustice perpetrated on one human being by another. When a bully picks on a child or we watch pictures of malnourished children on our TV screens, we feel a surge of emotion – the righteous anger that moves our hands and feet to take action.

If we look closely at the difference between our anger and God's anger, we quickly recognise that the big difference between the two is that *self* is present in our anger. God is self-*less* but we are so self-*more*; self-filled and so selfish. When we are filled with self, there is no room for God. And that selfishness is often the real root of our anger. We simply want things *our* way.

Aristotle said:

Anyone can be angry. That is easy.
But to be angry with the right person,
  To the right degree,
    at the right time,
      for the right person,
        and in the right way – that is not easy.

Revd Thomas Secker, in the seventeenth century, wrote: 'He that would be angry and not sin must be angry at nothing *but* sin' – acknowledging that we are to be angry about the sin rather than the sinner – the person; angry about their behaviour rather than angry about them as an individual: a unique individual worthy of God's grace and forgiveness and infinitely loved by Him.

That's a very different viewpoint to the one we usually hold when we're angry!

Understanding anger, finding its root and learning how it influences each of us will enable us to view anger with acceptance and grace.

ACTIVITY

Using a notebook and pen, write down any angry feelings you are aware of at the moment – both minor irritations and larger grievances.

Look at the Anger Mountain on page 120 to help you identify those feelings (we will use this chart in more depth later).

REFLECTION

Bring your feelings of anger – large and small, fleeting and long-standing – before God with honesty and humility.

Remind yourself that anger is a part of your being made in God's image. Ask God to show you where your anger is justified – and where He needs to teach you through it and move you on.

PRAYER

Father God, as I explore the nature of anger, give me a safe place – Your arms – in which to express my own anger, and help me to gain a wise perspective on the anger of others.

Prue, a friend of Chris, who has struggled with anger, wrote the following poem during a daily quiet time. Her emotions and responses are common to all of us. You may like to use her words for your own reflection.

Hot searing pain
anger volcanically erupting
burning passionate words
pouring out of my heart
destroying the world around me
killing all in its path.

Where can I go?
Where can I hide?
Who can soothe this pain?
Who can take this anger
and not be destroyed?

I run into the Father's arms
and spill the torment and the tears
in gobbets of anguish and rage
onto His breast
I feel His arms around me
stilling me as a mother stills her child.
I hear His voice.
My sobs subside
I am stilled.

CHAPTER 2

UNDERSTANDING ANGER

INTRODUCTION

Controlling our anger is a little like controlling the weeds in our garden or window box: just as trimming weeds at ground level will not stop them re-growing, it's not enough to 'trim' our anger by telling ourselves to stop getting angry or by trying hard to control our temper. Unless we also heave up the roots of weeds and find out where they came from, they will keep popping up in the most inconvenient places. We need to understand the roots – and route – of anger.

WHERE DOES ANGER COME FROM?

We are by nature sinful, fallen, human beings. The Bible states that we have all sinned and fall short of the glory of God (Rom. 3:23). Anger is part of that shortfall. That's not to justify our anger, but to acknowledge that because we are sinful people, the way we deal with anger is usually sinful. Our sinful nature will inevitably be linked to our weaknesses and vulnerabilities. When we are tired, ill, stressed, or under the pressure of demands and duties, anger is much more likely to get the better of us.

In those circumstances we will sometimes lose perspective, misconstrue a passing comment, deny a reasonable request, or misunderstand a straightforward situation. It all becomes 'too much' and we become angry.

Usually that anger has a self-focus: 'I can't cope with this any more'; 'Why is it always me who has to do this?'; 'What ARE you doing?'

Anger is often linked to loss. We become angry at a loss of love, of worth, of appreciation or respect. Injustice, unfairness, fear of failure and insecurity all feed angry feelings until they are fat enough to burst. And they frequently do.

At a basic personal level, anger is affected by a number of factors:

- our temperament
- ego
- personal strengths
- what we have learnt about anger from our family or upbringing
- our value system
- our religious experience

IN PRACTICE

YOUR ANGER PROFILE

Using a notebook and pen, compile your own anger profile by examining each of the factors opposite in detail:

- How would you – and others – describe your temperament?
- How do you view yourself? Are you confident? Capable? A good leader? A follower? Better than others at your job? Keen to learn? Slow to take initiative?
- What are your personal strengths? Patience? An ability to negotiate? Listening skills?
- What have you learnt about anger from your upbringing? What was your parents' attitude to anger? How was anger dealt with in your family as a child?
- What do you believe about anger generally? How do you react when someone you know/don't know becomes angry?
- What do you understand about anger where God is concerned? What do you believe the Bible teaches about anger?

Look at your 'profile' – are you surprised by anything you have written? Can you make connections between the anger you have experienced recently and the elements you have noted? What has this exercise taught you?

Anger is evident in various forms and even disguises. We may not admit to anger, but it will be there operating undercover. The Anger Mountain (Appendix, page 120) shows us just how anger builds and develops.

Anger is expressed both actively and passively. The passive expressions of anger usually remain inside, often busily gathering the evidence to help our anger 'case'. Active expressions are externally expressed, involving other people, situations or objects. Passive anger can quickly become active anger, and active anger can remain buried away, converted to passive anger, long after we have expressed it and believe we have dealt with it. Indeed, passive anger which finally erupts after being buried can erupt with more force and damage potential than anger that was actively expressed from the start.

It is we who are responsible for how we handle both types of anger. If we are calm and placid by nature we may not 'fly off the handle' but we may hide and harbour resentment beneath a veneer of quiet. Possessing an inflated sense of our own importance may make us more likely to become angry when someone else doesn't agree with our self-estimate. If a parent had a bad temper, we may have inherited it, or have been so appalled by the damage it did that we keep ourselves in check – not always with healthy results. Having been told that is it 'bad' to be angry and 'good' to put up with things we may be little more than a seething doormat!

If our own father was a punishing figure, we may transfer those attributes to God as our heavenly Father, only to live under the condemnation given by a distorted view of Him. Consequently, even our relationship with God will affect how angry we are.

The expectations and offerings of our culture and the everyday world we live in will also contribute to our level of anger. At extremes, we may be made impatient by a culture that suggests we can 'have it all', be lured to 'escape it all' with recreational drugs and their angry side-effects, or witness the anger of others escalate under the influence of alcohol. Yet even the simplest activities and circumstances can feed our anger: the school run, the mountain of ironing waiting for us at the end of a tiring day or even just the weather.

Anger is fickle too: what clouds our face with it on one day may not even suggest its passing shadow on another. That's because, as we will discover later, it is sometimes very much up to us to decide whether we will entertain anger beyond its first demanding appearance. We have a choice as well as a responsibility.

WHY DO WE BECOME ANGRY?

Our anger always has a focus, so understanding who or what we become angry with can help us understand the nature and source of angry feelings.

WE BECOME ANGRY WITH...

People	Things
God	Inanimate objects
Parents	Obstacles
Siblings	Difficulties
Our children	Injustice
Our friends	Unfairness
Our boss	Real threats
Those in authority	Perceived threats
Strangers	Inequality
Ourselves	
In relationship	**In abstract form**

If we were asked to choose the one 'thing' that makes us most deeply angry and most often, we would probably choose people!

It's inevitable that when we rub shoulders with human beings as flawed as we are on a daily basis, sooner or later we will irritate them – and be irritated by them.

People expect much of us; they crowd our space, overlook our needs and cause us all kinds of inconvenience, frustration and worry. And we do exactly the same to them!

We have already mentioned that what begins as an irritation quickly builds into full-blown anger, often gathering evidence and ammunition from incidents along the way.

Often our anger with other people is seriously misplaced, spreading its impact far beyond the person with whom we were originally angry.

Imagine this scenario: Our boss frustrates us during a working day, so we drive home in rush-hour traffic, angry with just about everyone on the road. We yell at the teenage daughter whose bag we trip over in the hallway and groan at the pile of breakfast dishes still in the sink. 'Whose job was it to wash those?' we wonder. Suddenly the whole family are on the receiving end of our quietly fuming anger as we attempt to control ourselves.

We open the post only to exclaim at the telephone bill and vow to unplug it permanently. There is no cheese to make the supper with, and even the fridge door gets an angry slam in protest. Then our husband walks through the door with a cheery smile and we are angry simply because he isn't: 'How dare you be so cheerful?' we snap. So our anger angers him and, as he leaves the kitchen after our frustrated outburst and 'woe is me' overture, it is the dog who gets the sharp end of our tongue as we shout at him, too, leaving him cowering in his basket.

If we stopped to measure the impact of that anger – originally meant for one man, our boss – we would discover that it had been felt by upwards of twenty people, and had been flung at several dozen more collectively.

We would recognise that it had also been directed at the people we love most, people we don't know at all, several motor vehicles, a roundabout, three sets of traffic lights, a telecoms company totalling several hundred employees, the telephone itself, some non-existent cheese, a fridge, a pile of unwashed crockery and a dog. Ludicrous, isn't it? That's the expansive power of anger!

Yet it's a scenario that we will probably know at least part of well, and one that will often leave us in tears as we ask, 'Why am I so angry?'

How are we to understand such anger?

A MODEL FOR UNDERSTANDING ANGER

It might be helpful to consider the following 'Anger Model' to help us understand how, why, when and what happens when we become angry.

AN ANGER MODEL

When we become angry we follow a pathway of four As.

- Arousal – by a trigger, hurt or fear.
- Appraisal – asks 'How shall I react?'
- Approval – asks, 'Is this justified? Yes! So do it!'
- Action – we do it.

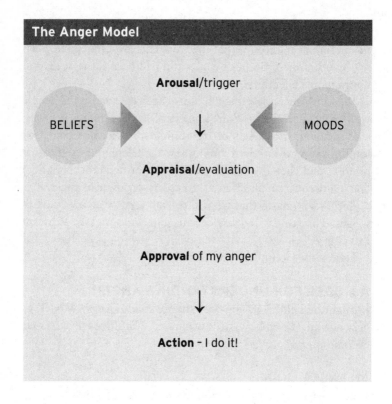

The Anger Model

Arousal/trigger

BELIEFS   MOODS

Appraisal/evaluation

Approval of my anger

Action - I do it!

Anger always begins with arousal or a trigger: an immediate incident, a memory of a past hurt, a digging up of old wounds – something that reminds us that anger can often be more *historical* than *hysterical*!

What we do at the moment of arousal or trigger, and how we appraise our uncomfortable feelings, will determine the nature of our anger and the path it will take.

We quickly evaluate and appraise anger in two ways, taking a bifocal view:

1. Through a lens coloured by our inner core beliefs – in spite of what has been said or done, we evaluate the trigger via these beliefs, regardless of whether these beliefs are true or false.
2. Through a lens coloured by our mood – the view affected by whether we are tired, stressed, tense, calm, low, hungry, optimistic, etc.

If we are low – physically or emotionally – we will be vulnerable to anger and more likely to approve the anger mood as it approaches. If we are feeling buoyed up and all is right with our world, we will be more likely to face up to the anger, see it for what it is and not give it a welcome as we don't want our equilibrium spoiled.

UNDERSTANDING TRIGGERS

Understanding what arouses or 'triggers' our anger is the first step to giving it the kind of welcome it deserves.

TRIGGERS

There are three main categories of anger triggers … you'll recognise the examples all too well!

Irritants: the daily irritants of life that injure us.

- A pile of dirty crockery and cutlery is left unwashed.
- A shop assistant is rude and unhelpful.
- The 'boys' in the house constantly leave the toilet seat up!

Costs: triggers involving loss.

- A child loses a school coat when the budget is tight.
- A partner contradicts us at a dinner party, costing us loss of face.
- We're asked to do something extra, unexpectedly losing time in a busy day.

Breaking of personal rules: when someone else breaks what are important personal rules for us – a transgression.

- Someone parks in 'our' parking space.
- A policy is passed at work that we don't agree with but have to abide by.
- A parent lets their children run riot in the supermarket: 'Our children would *never* have been allowed to behave like that!'

Another more hidden cause of anger is the arousal that occurs when something happens to link our current emotions with past hurts. A childhood experience of pain or humiliation from a long ago yesterday will be brought to the surface by similarities in pain or humiliation today, simply because that earlier hurt has never been dealt with. When this happens, we are matching the painful pattern of our childhood – and it makes us angry. It's as if part of us is trying to defend the inner child that is still hurting after all these years.

IN PRACTICE

PLOTTING THE TRIGGERS

This exercise requires commitment and a real desire to get to the bottom of our anger.

- Keep a small notebook close by throughout the day.
- Make a brief note each time you feel even a flicker of anger.
- Write what happened and how you felt, and then identify the trigger for that anger.

For example: 'Jane phoned, asking me if I could take her children to school – again. I felt used and put upon.'

Triggers: loss of time: 'I have a busy day'; loss of significance: 'I am being taken for granted'; breaking of personal rules: 'I can get out to take my children to school when I have a toddler – why can't Jane?'

At the end of the day, reflect on what has happened. What are the major triggers?

Bring those triggers before God in prayer and resolve to be aware of them – without loading yourself with guilt. Remember, we are flawed human beings.

We can also use this exercise to help others identify their anger (usually with their permission) or to help ourselves to deal with their anger.

If we consistently face the same kind of angry outbursts from a teenage daughter, examining when and how they happen may help us to defuse the anger or approach the issue differently. (It might be best if she doesn't discover – at least initially – that we are making a note of her outbursts!)

For example, we may note that her angry outbursts come as a result of us trying to curb her independence (a blocked goal – see the next section).

It may rightfully be time for us to make steps to extend the boundaries we set or reach some kind of mutually acceptable compromise. That's not to 'give in' but to examine whether her blocked goals are inappropriately blocked.

UNDERSTANDING THE SIGNIFICANCE OF PERSONAL GOALS

Personal goals are important. We are made in God's image, so it follows that He would give us motivation to choose to work towards goals, just as He does. We may work towards riding a bike, a degree, a business achievement, painting the spare room or managing to cook our first ever roast dinner. Other goals may be more subtle: financial independence, recognition, esteem, fame. Our days are filled with short- and long-term goals which represent progress and achievement to us.

Sometimes our goals are unclear or not easily apparent. They may remain hidden or unacknowledged until they are blocked in some way: a need to feel valued or respected, perhaps. That's when we become angry.

Meet Gerald.

Gerald has an important business meeting on Friday for which he wants to look smart. He had asked his wife Sue several times over the previous weekend if she would arrange to have his best suit dry-cleaned before Friday, as her route to work passes the door of the dry-cleaner.

On Tuesday evening, Gerald discovers that she has forgotten, so he gently reminds her. On Wednesday evening he finds the suit hanging in the wardrobe, still waiting to be cleaned. His stressful day, and worry about the meeting, triggers an angry outburst as follows ...

Arousal/Trigger
'My wife doesn't do what I ask her.'
↓
Beliefs affecting appraisal of situation
'If Sue loved me then she would do what I ask.'
↓
Anger (blocked goal)
To feel loved
↓
Action
Gerald loses it and rants and raves at Sue:
'Don't you want me to get this contract?!'
↓
Sue's arousal/trigger
Gerald out of control.
↓

Continued overleaf ...

↓

Beliefs affecting appraisal of situation
Sue: 'If I don't retaliate it's safer, so I will retreat inside
myself for safety. I'm to blame, I'm no good.'

↓

Anger (blocked goal)
To feel appreciated

↓

Action
Sue: Depression
And because she is depressed, she forgets the suit yet again.
Friday morning – the number two suit is worn to the
business meeting.

Gerald: 'It'll be all her fault if this goes badly.'
Sue: 'It'll be all my fault if this goes badly.'

Hidden goals are important to identify because they can shed
a great deal of light on the reasons for our anger. Anger occurs
when our goal is blocked, because our deepest needs are not
being met in God, but in the reaching of our own goals.

A hidden goal raises the questions:

- Who am I trying to please?
- Why do I drive myself in this way?
- What is my motivation?
- What do I expect to get out of this?

IN PRACTICE

THE CONCERT

Back to the teenage daughter (who is a never-ending source of inspiration for handling anger!). Consider the following scenario as an exercise in identifying hidden goals that are in danger of being blocked.

An argument arises because daughter wants to miss an afternoon of school to get to an evening concert in a nearby city with friends. Mum says that she must not miss school in her A level year, for whatever reason.

Daughter maintains that she must get there early to get in and that missing two free periods and a double block of English is not crucial.

Mum's hidden goals: *significance*: daughter must do well at A levels to get into university; *security*: 'I worry – and anyway, I must be in control of this situation – not my daughter'; *self-worth*: mum angry that her values are not apparently shared or respected by daughter.

Daughter's hidden goals: *significance*: 'I must go to this concert or look "sad" in front of my friends'; *independence/self-worth*: 'Mum doesn't realise that I can do the reading and get the notes later – she doesn't trust me!'

- How might applying the questions above help mother and daughter resolve their issues – in theory if not in practice?!

We learn certain goal-setting behaviour from an early age and develop our own strategies for linking goals to self-worth, security and significance.

Meet Ian.

Ian is the youngest of four children of a lone parent. His mother was emotionally distant as a result of her loss. She was also anxious that she should provide for her children, give them a Christian upbringing, and help 'set them up for life'.

Because of her busyness, Ian had to fight for her attention from a young age and soon learnt that because of his mother's strong work ethic, the harder he worked and the better he did at school, the more she gave him attention.

If he succeeded, she would say, 'Well done. That's really good.' The rest of the time, her busyness meant that he felt more or less ignored.

Ian began to make connections in his mind: 'If I work hard and do well at school, my mother will give me attention.' This attention fed Ian's self-worth. As a result, he began to develop a perfectionist attitude, because when he was 'perfect' he was loved.

This flawed connection strengthened as Ian's perfectionism increased and he began to drive himself hard. Instead of seeking his sense of value and worth through the eyes of God, he relied entirely on his mother's assessment.

Even in his perfectionist adult life Ian continued to try to be 'perfect'. Now he was working not just in order to please his mother, but because he had learnt that this was the way to keep his self-esteem raised. His mantra became: 'The harder I work the more approval I earn and the more love – and self-love – I have.'

Ian worked hard and did well at work, earning the approval and praise of his boss. His perfectionism worked for him as he met his goal: perfection leading to approval and self-esteem.

When the company Ian worked for was restructured, his boss promised that he would be given promotion under a new team leader. But when the new boss arrived, his approach was very different. A demanding bully, the new boss dismissed the promise of promotion and told Ian that he was useless. Whatever Ian did, even though it was as good as, if not better than, before, did not please the new boss, who wanted to maintain power. Ian was denied approval and missed out on promotion.

His self-esteem plummeted, he became confused and dis-oriented. He started to crumble inside because his 'goal' was not working for him. He became increasingly angry with himself for not being good enough and angry with his boss for not understanding his goal. An already difficult relationship deteriorated.

Ian's *goal* – to be successful through promised promotion in order to feel worth.

His *blocked goal* – the new boss told him he wasn't good enough for promotion.

His *thoughts* – 'I ought to have got promotion: I must be a hopeless failure because I didn't.'

The *result* – Ian was very angry with himself, his boss – and with God.

All behaviour moves towards a goal. Ian's goal caused him to be angry because it became a blocked goal.

GOAL
(In order to quench thirst)
Achieve success
through promotion

→ Thirst to feel valued
and significant by
achieving

BLOCKED GOAL
Boss didn't give him
promotion

THOUGHTS
I ought to have got
promotion. I'm a
hopeless failure
because I didn't.

EMOTION
Anger – with self, his
boss and God

If Ian had recognised that his work was as good as ever, he would have been able to detach himself from the criticism. He could have learnt to handle his anger and address his disappointment by recognising his attempt to meet deep needs through his success and the approval of others, rather than through God's unconditional acceptance of him and his work.

More than anything, Ian needed to recognise that God values him regardless of his success. That he is worth so much that God paid a sacrificial price for him. If he had gradually learnt and understood that certainty in small ways as he grew up, assimilating it into his values and beliefs, he may still not have had 'success' as he saw it, but the negative impact would have been less as his self-worth would have been rooted in a secure place: God. Such deep-rooted anger and disappointment could have been avoided and Ian would have been able to see his situation for what it was: an insecure bully making a victim of a hard-working employee he saw as a threat.

God has created us with a thirst to be secure, to know self-worth and to feel significant. He intends us to have that thirst quenched ultimately by His unconditional love and acceptance.

However, our first knowledge of such love and acceptance will – or should – come from our family. When we are born into a family, we are born with an empty emotional tank, into which, hopefully, our parents will pour a sense of security, self-worth and significance.

Our levels of security, self-worth and significance might remain low because we don't experience good parenting. Perhaps we are never told, 'You are a wonderful daughter' or 'I love you'.

Ian had never heard his mother say, 'You are very special. It doesn't matter how successful you are, how good at school you are. I love you because you are you.' He thought he was only lovable because of how well he did or how successful he was.

None of our emotional tanks will be filled to the brim or filled consistently and abundantly, because none of us has known perfect parenting. How we live with various levels in our emotional tank will also depend, to some extent, on our personality, and on how much we have felt that tank topped up as we have grown from a child into an adult. Various life experiences may drain that tank – a difficult adolescence perhaps – and we may reach adulthood still 'thirsty' for approval and esteem.

Ian was still thirsting, even as an adult, because he had not found the right source of love, approval and esteem. He had moved towards his goal to be perfect, to be successful, because when he felt perfect and successful he knew worth. When his goal was blocked, his emotional tank was drained to the last drop. When Ian thought he was not doing something perfectly and earning approval he did not feel worthwhile. With his goal blocked and with no way to reach it within the estimation of his new boss, who stood in its way, Ian became angry. Anger is always, in some way or another, the result of a blocked goal.

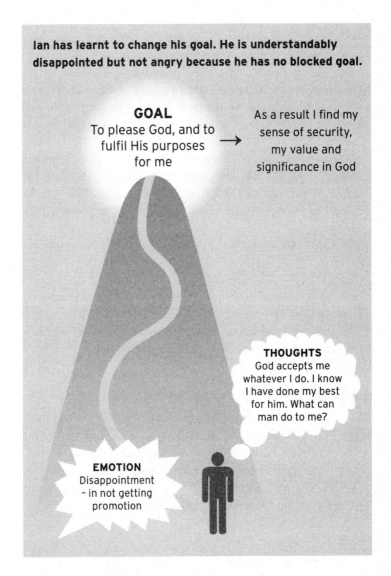

55

'The chief end of man is to worship God and enjoy Him forever', says the Shorter Westminster Catechism.

Our goal is to please God and be in relationship with Him. When we are moving towards that goal our emotional tanks are full whatever happens, because we are secure in our relationship with God the Father whose love is unconditional, constant and grace-filled.

Ian could be helped to see that his worth is not dependent upon being perfect and successful, but comes from the fact that Someone loves him so much that He would die for him, *did* die for him, and that his value lies in who he is, not in what he does.

IN PRACTICE

GOAL SETTING FOR IAN

• How would you help Ian to reset his goals and move towards them, taking into account his disappointment, his learned behaviour and the significance, self-worth and security – the hope – offered by the new God-centred model?

Sometimes we simply set goals for ourselves that are too hard, too rigid – even unachievable. God wants us to set challenging goals for ourselves, but He wants us to remember that we are only human – our goals need to be flexible.

Chris tells an amusing story of how her less-than-perfect typing forced her to make her goal a more flexible one:

I was PA for George Carey in Durham which involved typing the Sunday notice sheet. Obviously I used to do my best and check for mistakes. But on so many occasions on a Sunday I found that instead of typing 'Christ's body' or 'Christ's Church', I had printed 'Chris's body' and 'Chris's Church'! On another occasion I typed 'come to the BBQ at the Vicarave'. BIG mistakes!

My sense of self-esteem went wobbling down and my goal to be successful was well and truly blocked – I was furious with myself. How could I do such a thing? I could cope with not being perfect but I wanted to be successful. I used to sit in church and feel awful because of my 'blocked goal'. In the end I had to really take myself in hand and say 'Hang on a minute, Chris. You are here because God has given you this job. He knows you are not perfect. He knows you can't spell but He has given you a significant place to be. So if it's good enough for God it's good enough for you.' I really had to work hard, not so much at the spelling, but at changing my goal and making it more flexible.

God wants us to do our very best for Him. But He wants us to do so within the context of the loving, accepting, relationship we have with Him. That means ensuring that our goals are flexible enough to be accommodated within that relationship of unconditional love and acceptance: a relationship based on love which loves us *anyway*, whether we reach our goals or not. That's not to devalue our goals or dismiss them as unimportant – but to recognise that the love of God is greater, higher, wider than any goal we set ourselves. In fact, God Himself *is* our ultimate goal.

Our first goal as Christians is to enjoy God, to have a life of worship and to relate to Him in an ever deeper way. We need to understand that we are a much loved and lovable people in His sight and to recognise that our sense of worth and significance lies first and foremost in God.

God delights in our successes and achievements and celebrates with us – but He delights in our relationship with Him so much more. Understanding that He is our ultimate goal and that a closer relationship with Him is the way to meet that goal may in turn defuse much of our anger.

However, damage may have already been done.

The next part of the book examines what anger actually does to us and how we can deal with its impact and results.

ACTIVITY

What sort of unrealistic and unhelpful goals do you set yourself?

Use a notebook and pen for the following exercise.

Think of a recent event which made you angry – perhaps something that happened today, so that you can remember it clearly.

First: Identify which of your goals was blocked. Was it significance when someone else got the credit? Control – when an agenda was changed?

Second: Recognise that perhaps you were depending more on reaching this goal for a sense of security, a feeling of belonging, self-worth or significance, rather than trusting in God's estimation of your position.

Third: Identify what you were saying to yourself about the situation that caused your anger.

Fourth: What do you need to relearn about your place before God in the light of this experience? What mental note or picture can you make to use as a memo next time you are in this situation?

REFLECTION

Reflect on some of the new thoughts this activity has presented to you.

Bring them before God and ask Him to help you to understand the way in which blocked goals are so often the root – and route – of your anger.

Ask Him to forgive you for any resentment that remains and to help you to draw closer to Him in the loving, accepting, gracious relationship He longs for: a relationship which will ultimately meet your deepest needs.

PRAYER

Father God, You are waiting for me to find my security and worth in You. Yet so often I wrench that assurance away from You in my own independence and need for control. Please show me that You are the source of all my security, all my self-worth and all my significance. I am a child of the King! I am loved unconditionally! You are my ultimate goal and I am safe in Your arms for eternity.

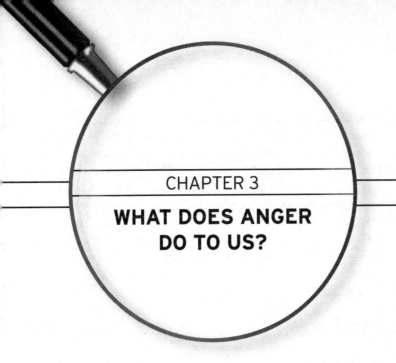

CHAPTER 3

WHAT DOES ANGER DO TO US?

INTRODUCTION

Anger, as we have discovered, is a signal: a behaviour change which alerts us to the fact that our goal is blocked.

Yet anger doesn't happen in neat or contained isolation. It affects almost every area of our lives, impacting not just our emotions but our bodies and our mental and spiritual health. First and foremost, anger influences our behaviour, dictating the way that we react to events and circumstances, encouraging attitudes and actions in response. Exploring the relationship between anger and behaviour helps us to understand the explosive potential of their close relationship and what we can do to keep that relationship on an even keel.

ANGER AND BEHAVIOUR

Anger can influence behaviour in ways that are passive: moodiness, sulks and silences; or aggressive: tantrums, door slamming, shouting and threats. We can be helped to understand that influence by considering different kinds of anger as if they were personified and given a human character of their own.

So, meet the extended 'Angry family'. Although we have used titles: Miss, Mr, Mrs, etc – these are not patterns of anger exclusive to male or female, neither are they intended to typecast a particular sex. Every one of us has the potential to be anger personified!

THE ANGRY FAMILY

Miss Manipulator

As a child, Miss Manipulator would hold her breath, scream as loud as she could, and lie on the floor kicking in order to get her own way. As an angry adult she uses tears to manipulate others to do what she wants, or uses headaches or illnesses in order to get out of their way – or keep them out of hers.

Mr Hang-out

As a child, Mr Hang-out used to hold his breath and scream like Miss Manipulator. As an adult he still enjoys shouting and screaming at everyone and everything and expresses his anger through adult temper tantrums, letting his anger 'hang out'.

Miss Blamer

Miss Blamer projects her anger onto others. It's always 'everyone else's fault' because she hasn't done anything wrong. She angrily blames everyone and everything, refusing to take any responsibility for her anger.

Mr Stuffer

Mr Stuffer is not in touch with his anger. He has stuffed it down so far inside himself that he can't see it. His anger is so deeply buried that he feels numb and is unable to feel it.

Miss Silence

Miss Silence is an expert at not speaking. As soon as she feels angry, she says, 'I don't want to talk about it' and retreats to a place of silence, unable or unwilling to express her angry feelings.

Master Moody

Master Moody uses the same tactics as Miss Silence, but everyone knows when Master Moody is angry because his silence is accompanied by pouts and huffs and his face and body language send out angry messages.

Ms Volcano

Ms Volcano finds it difficult to express anger, so she stockpiles grievances pushing them beneath the surface for storage. Suddenly, something (often something quite small) triggers an eruption and she 'blows her top', pouring out a stinking, smouldering lava of words and fury.

Miss Daydreamer

Like Ms Volcano, Miss Daydreamer doesn't like to express her anger so she escapes into her mind and replays that anger and the hurt accompanying it. In her imagination she sees herself telling others that she is hurt and angry, acting out a scene to her own satisfaction. But she would never dare to do that in reality. She is too nice to say anything.

Mr Fearful

Mr Fearful is afraid of what others might think of him if he became angry. He has a real fear that if he attempts to express his anger, he will lose control. He feels guilty about his anger and is not sure God will forgive his feelings of resentment.

Mrs Controller

Mrs Controller likes to control people like objects, rather than relating to them. She is angry when she is unable to control others, because she feels insecure.

Mr Emotional-Junkie

Mr Emotional-Junkie believes the meaning of life lies in creating a buzz around himself, whether from alcohol, drugs, sex or getting angry. His behaviour is a way of getting away from the frustrations and irritations of life that feed his anger – even though he often gets a buzz from feeling that way.

Miss Martyr

Miss Martyr blames herself for anything and everything that happens in her life so that all her anger is self-directed – often with dangerous or tragic results.

We may recognise ourselves – and others – amongst the Angry family. Each of us has the potential to become any one of them at any moment – or even two or three at a time!

Understanding which members of the family our anger most resembles can help us understand our own behaviour.

IN PRACTICE

FAMILY RESEMBLANCES
- Which members of the Angry family do you notice that you have more than a passing resemblance to?
- Do you share family traits with more than two or three?
- How does it make you feel to recognise yourself amongst this gathering?
- What might you do as a result?

ANGER AND OUR BODIES

When we get angry, we begin to notice our anger being expressed physically in our bodies. Our muscles may tense, we may feel butterflies in our stomach, begin to shake, sweat or feel the onset of a headache. This physical discomfort is often the first indication that anger is rising.

We will then usually experience what is called a 'flight or fight' response.

The fight or flight response proceeds as follows:

- When we experience an emotional arousal of anger the autonomic nervous system is triggered.
- The sympathetic nervous system releases the hormone adrenalin, which prepares the body for fight or flight.
- An extra supply of the hormone adrenalin is secreted and distributed.

- Our heart beats more rapidly.
- Our blood pressure rises.
- Respiration deepens and increases.
- The pupils dilate.
- Our voice becomes louder.
- Speech quickens.
- The sympathetic nervous system diverts blood from the skin, stomach and intestines to the heart, central nervous system and muscles, because the body is preparing for action. (The reason why some people get stomach upsets in response to anger.)
- We often lose our appetite – or sometimes make straight for the biscuit tin!
- We have a desire to yell out.
- We know a strong desire to move limbs forcefully and quickly.

Candace Pert has contributed to our understanding that emotions are active biochemical agents. In her book *Molecule of Emotion*[1] she writes:

> It's true, we do store some memory in the brain, but by far, the deeper, older messages are stored in the body and must be accessed through the body. Your body is your subconscious mind and you can't heal it by talk alone.

Our body and mind work in close partnership and will often give each other a signal to help us deal with situations faced by either or both. Becoming aware of our bodies and how they react to either the creeping onset of anger or its full-blown assault can be a crucial first-line action in attempting to control it.

There is a discipline and wisdom in training ourselves to stop momentarily in our tracks to ask, 'What is this anger saying?'

ANGER AND OUR THOUGHTS

How we view the triggers that cause anger, and what they mean to us, will determine the intensity of our anger. If we take a hostile view of something, then it will become a trigger for anger. If we view it tolerantly and benignly it will not.

These views are modelled by our 'self-talk', the things we say to ourselves about the situation we are facing: our justification of our anger; the dialogue and defence our 'inner lawyer' keeps up on our behalf.

For example:

A businessman is kept waiting in the hospital outpatient department and gets really angry.

His self-talk says: 'I am a busy and important man – don't they realise that I have a job to do? This is totally unacceptable! It says here in the patient charter that the waiting time should be no longer than thirty minutes – I've been here thirty-five! What kind of business are they running here?!'

If he could stop and check his anger, and check his self-talk before it begins, he might respond by saying: 'This is a different environment to my office environment. Agendas have to be flexible here – there are ill people involved and illness is unpredictable. It's important that they are given time. I might learn from that!

'The waiting time is thirty minutes – well, I've only been here thirty-five, not too bad so far. I can spend this time working on my laptop anyway – and there are fewer interruptions than at the office.'

IN PRACTICE

SELF-TALK

In your notebook, write down the negative self-talk that leads to anger and the more positive, rational self-talk that might keep it at bay for each of the following scenarios:

- A woman gets angry when her husband always comes home late from work. What is her negative self-talk? What could she say to herself to change her self-talk to help her keep her anger at bay?
- A man gets angry when his boss at work constructively criticises his team. What is his negative self-talk? What could he tell himself in order to cope positively with this constructive criticism?
- A mother hits the roof in anger when her daughter comes in late. What is she really saying to herself? To her daughter? What could she say to herself to help manage her anger more appropriately?

Our thoughts are very powerful, triggering our moods and responses. How we evaluate our reaction to something can set off a trail of thought that either leads us away from anger – or deeper into anger, self-doubt, self-pity or depression.

We can subconsciously indulge in irrational self-talk which encourages us to believe evidence that is unfounded but which contributes to our anger: 'Well, he doesn't love me anyway'; 'I can't do this, can I? I'm useless at everything'; 'They never invite me to join their team so they must think I am bad at my job.'

The result of listening to our own self-talk is that we become increasingly angry at our blocked goals. We involve others – and ourselves – in that blockage by adding to it out of our (usually misguided) beliefs about what it is that is actually getting in the way of those goals.

At the level of our subconscious self-talk, we speak to ourselves at 1,500 words a minute – three times faster than normal conversation. No wonder we build up so much negative evidence to fuel our anger! Our self-talk builds a bonfire of evidence, adding piece by piece to the pile until our anger is ready to ignite the dry tinder – then, bang!

Our self-deception and misinterpretation of events and words often play a larger part in anger than we realise.

It's very important for us when we are trying to understand our own anger – or, when we are working with others, to help them understand their own – to identify the thoughts which attach themselves to anger. They may have no right to form such an attachment.

ANGER AND OUR BELIEFS

Random thoughts very quickly become beliefs, but beliefs influence our anger –positively or negatively – in other ways.

Often our own personal value systems help us weigh up our anger and tell us whether it is justified or not, giving us tools to appraise that anger so that it fits, or dictates, our rules for living:

Appraisal: My mother's anger was very frightening.
Belief: Anger is frightening.
Rule for living: If I make people angry, then it will be
                    frightening.
                    (Conclusion: I try not to make people angry.)

Appraisal: I live at No.10 and the Leader of the
                    Opposition wants to move here.
Belief: My days are numbered.
Rule for living: If I keep smiling, then people will like me.
                    (Conclusion: Smiling keeps me in No.10.)

IN PRACTICE

BELIEFS AND RULES

To understand this pattern and to help identify it in your own thinking, try establishing the conclusions for the following beliefs:

Appraisal: If I expressed anger as a child, I was
                    told I was stupid.
Belief: I am stupid.
Rule for living: If I don't express anger then I will
                    not be seen as stupid.
                    Conclusion_____

Appraisal: My uncle's anger was out of control and
                    he got his own way.
Belief: Anger = getting own way.
Rule for living: If I get angry then I feel in control.
                    Conclusion_____

Appraisal:	If I was compliant, bit my lip and kept my mouth shut, I wasn't hit.
Belief:	It's better not to retaliate.
Rule for living:	When people get angry with me, it is better I am silent and retreat into an inside world – no one can reach me inside.
	Conclusion _____

Appraisal:	My mother always gave me attention when I got angry.
Belief:	Anger is good.
Rule for living:	If I get angry then I feel important and strong.
	Conclusion _____

• Can you identify the belief and rule for living that feeds your anger?

Appraisal:	_____
Belief:	_____
Rule for living:	If _____
	Then _____

The problem with this system, of course, is that we don't always get it *right*: we make errors in appraising our anger and it is important that we recognise a tendency to do so. We need to be able to identify the errors in our thinking if we are to handle anger in a healthy and well-balanced way.

Identifying thinking errors:
We make mistakes in our appraisal of our own thinking and belief formation in various ways:

1. Selective perception
Occurs when we only notice one aspect of the situation we are facing and choose to become blinkered to other relevant information.

2. 'Mind-reading'
Happens when we assume what somebody else in the situation is thinking without checking that assumption out. We may base whole plans of action on what we believe is real and true behaviour when it is only our unfounded assumption.

3. Awfulising
Is when we tell ourselves, 'This is absolutely awful ...', blowing the situation up out of all proportion. If we were able to stand back and see a situation clearly for what it really is our reaction wouldn't be so bad. It's what we so often call not being able 'to see the wood for the trees'.

4. Emotive language
When we describe an event or action in emotive language, we will inevitably 'fire ourselves' up by using words and phrases such as: 'disaster', 'betrayed', 'for the rest of my life', 'it's the last time', etc. This will frame a situation in terms of that language.

5. Over-generalising
Occurs when we notice that something is true but go over the

top in our interpretation of that situation. If someone has let us down and we feel angry, we may over-generalise to add weight to our 'case' by saying, 'He *always* lets me down', when in reality it might only be the first time. Or we conclude that someone in the street ignored us when they just forgot their contact lenses.

IN PRACTICE

FLAGGING ERRORS
- As you read through the thinking errors listed above, did you recognise any of your own thinking errors?
- What can you do to 'flag up' the error danger in an anger situation?

ANGER AND MOODS

Our mood, like our thinking patterns and beliefs, can influence nearly every area of our lives. If it were possible, we might face the same challenges and circumstances on two different days and yet deal with those days and those circumstances differently, depending entirely on our mood.

The major influences on our mood are:

- Our state of health
- The regularity of the physical exercise we take
- Adequate nutrition and diet
- The consumption of certain drugs – alcohol and tobacco included
- The quality of our sleep
- Quality time for relaxation

- The level of stress in our life
- Social factors – environment, family, work, relationships

Just recognising those factors and acknowledging our vulnerability to mood-related anger can help us take preventative steps to avoid it.

ANGER AND GOD

Anger is not divorced from our faith or excluded from our relationship with God. We do not stop being angry because we have faith in God. Yet, often we are surprised by the intensity of our anger despite that faith. It is important, therefore, that we explore and understand what anger can do to and for us – negatively and positively – in the context of our relationship with God.

Almost all of us will have known times when we have recognised feelings of anger towards God. We may have shouted, 'Where are You, God?' or asked in desperation, 'I don't understand, Lord – what are You doing?'

Anger can rock our faith or produce slow, creeping cracks more than any other emotion. We may *know* that even when we cannot fathom the *actions* of God, we need to trust His *character*, but we don't *feel* that way.

Our anger is not to be dismissed or buried because it is an expression of our honesty: what God wants with us more than anything is an honest relationship.

So how do we best manage our honest anger in an honest relationship with God?

Many of the problems we have in relation to anger and God come from our own mistaken beliefs about His view of our anger, or a distortion of our experience and learning which have contributed to those beliefs.

When we are angry with God, we may believe any of the following:

- 'It's dangerous to be angry with God – He'll punish me.'
  From: a mistaken view of God as a punishing Father figure.
- 'It's unfair to be angry with God – He's too busy; He's perfect; I can't taint him with my rubbish.'
  From: a mistaken view of God as disinterested, rejecting the intimacy with us that He longs for.
- 'It's pointless to be angry with God – I deserve everything I get anyway.'
  From: a mistaken view of God as vengeful when we are in a place of low self-worth.
- 'My anger has to go somewhere – it's safest to throw it at God.'
  A healthy initial response that acknowledges God's refuge as a place of unconditional love, protection and safety.
- 'It's safe to express my angry feelings – God can hold them.'
  A healthy acknowledgement that God is bigger than any anger we can throw at Him.

Between the lines of these reactions emerges the question asked by every Christian: 'Can I be angry with God?' The answer is, 'Yes!' because anger is a very human reaction to pain, helplessness and bewilderment. God expects it of us.

When we can't make sense of what's going on, we hurt inside or we are frightened about what might happen, we will often throw our resulting angry feelings at God – and that's exactly what He wants us to do.

God knows our hearts and minds. He knows how we feel. It is safer to throw our anger at One who has intimate knowledge of us, and who absorbs it all, than anyone else – even ourselves.

God is bigger than all of it.

As news broke of the tragedy of the school shootings at Dunblane, Scotland in March 1996, Steve Chalke, then working with GMTV, was hurriedly sent to Scotland with co-broadcaster Lorraine Kelly to cover the event and to try to give some kind of faith perspective on the horror facing that small town.

In the course of their report, Lorraine Kelly, shocked and bewildered, and no doubt echoing the emotions and words of every viewer, turned to an equally shocked and bewildered Steve and said, 'An awful lot of people are very angry with God right now, Steve.'

To which Steve replied, 'That's OK. He can take it – His shoulders are broad enough.'

This was not the time for religiosity, glib comfort or any kind of effort at understanding, but merely for honest anger. Steve's words gave every GMTV viewer the space and freedom to be honest with God – whoever or whatever they believed Him to be. In doing so, he offered a tiny crumb of comfort and hope together with an understanding that there was a God who was listening. A God who could take our anger in the midst of our not understanding, because He is a God who more than anything wants relationship – and honesty in relationship.

Steve might have gone on to say that God was actually far more angry, appalled, hurt and saddened than the thousands of TV viewers about what had happened in Dunblane Primary School that morning. That He shared their disbelief, horror and pain. Consequently, the next question that might have been asked, and the one we inevitably ask ourselves in the light of such incomprehensible tragedy, is 'Why didn't God stop it happening?'

So often we angrily ask, 'Why doesn't God do something?' 'Why can't he make it all right?' 'Where was God in this?' At such times, we may rail against the heavens and find them silent. Silent, perhaps, because any answer would be just too big or too deep for us to understand. And even if we were given the opportunity to try to understand, our limited comprehension would begin a series of other questions and cries.

There is nothing new in these cries – or in the silence. Jesus Himself cried: 'My God, my God, why have you forsaken me?' (Matt. 27:46) We are in good company when we cry out in such a way. The Bible is full of characters that asked 'Why?', crying heavenward in despair and pain

Job was one such man. Utterly bewildered by the onslaught of troubles he faced, troubles which seemed to have occurred for no apparent reason, Job was honest before God in heartfelt prayer.

Eugene Peterson in his introduction to the book of Job (*The Message*), writes:

> Job suffered. His name is synonymous with suffering. He asked, 'Why?', he asked, 'Why me?' And he put his questions to God. He asked his questions persistently, passionately and eloquently. He refused to take silence for an answer. He refused to take clichés for an answer. He refused to let God off the hook.'[2]

It was the common understanding in the Old Testament that good behaviour would bring its own reward. Therefore, disobedient, rebellious behaviour would result in punishment. Job's friends took that line and said, 'This is happening to you because you have done all these things wrong.' But Job knew that he was beyond reproach. Even God had remarked to Satan, 'Have you considered my servant Job?' (Job 1:8).

Yet Job was left bewildered. The worst of his pain was not the suffering or the loss, but the lack of understanding and the unanswered question 'Why?'.

It's an age-old, timeless, universal question. Perhaps it's the very reason why the book of Job is included in the Bible.

But we can ask the question 'Why?' for years and never know the answer. It roots us to the spot and we are unable to move on. Sometimes we have to learn to live – albeit sadly or painfully – with unanswered questions, accepting that we will never know the answers to the question 'Why?' this side of eternity. Often, when we accept that we won't know – even that we don't *need* to know – we are at last able to move on.

The Psalms also are full of anger honestly expressed. David was an expert at honesty: 'Why, O LORD, do you stand far off? Why do you hide yourself in times of trouble?' (Psa. 10:1); 'How long, O LORD …' (Psa. 13:1–2).

David expressed his anger as 'I feel like this' and 'Life's not fair!' but he almost always moved on through 'but' or 'yet' to a place where he was able to acknowledge God's sovereignty and greatness and worship Him. David moved on despite his anger. He focused not on what was making him angry, on the 'Why?'s or related questions, but on the greater character of the God he knew he could trust 'whatever'.

Sometimes it can be helpful to use the psalmists' model to express our anger.

Both Chris and Wendy have known the desperation that leads to the writing of very personal psalms.

When Chris's daughter was very ill and weak with ME, remaining so despite constant prayer for intervention, Chris wrote her own heartfelt psalm:

You say you are compassionate –
where is your compassion?
You reached out and healed people –
don't you see my daughter?
What's wrong with her?
Why do you bless others and not her?
Yes, you are standing there …
Looking on and strengthening us …
But not intervening.
I feel angry.
You wonderfully bless and intervene in other lives
But not my daughter's.
YET, I will praise you.
You are the Father of all creation.
You created her in my womb
You have given her life and laughter.
You see all things from the beginning to the end.
Your ways aren't my ways
BUT you are my God, the King
And I will bless you and thank you
In everything.[3]

When Wendy was diagnosed with a second totally unrelated cancer just a few weeks after the six-year 'all clear' mark from a first cancer she wrote:

If I could write graffiti on the walls that curve around my path to
    heaven,
It would read 'No comfort.'
Even for those who love and trust in you.
'There is no comfort.'
Only the blackness of the night
And the emptiness of my heart
'There is no comfort.'
Only my dreams of longing to be held.
'There is no comfort.'
Though I cry out against the wall, the dark, the tears, even the
    dreams
Through the long watches of the night
'THERE IS NO COMFORT!'[14]

(Notice that, at the point of psalm writing, Chris was at a slightly
healthier point than Wendy where 'moving on' was concerned!
But Wendy did move forward in trust before too long!)

Not all of us find accepting anger or expressing it honestly such
a straightforward act. Some of us will have grown up in a family
situation where anger was effectively banned: 'We don't get
angry in this family.' Someone who has been taught to hide their
anger will keep it under wraps. They literally daren't be angry,
they daren't be real, and they will need specific help to be able to
acknowledge anger and to understand that expressing it is OK.

If we can come to a place of honesty when we are angry with
God, it can ensure that we are not left feeling angry forever. We
can move on in our relationship with Him and establish again
who He is, and what His plan for us is, in relation to our 'present

sufferings' (Rom. 8:18). We learn again to fix our eyes on His character rather than His unfathomable actions – or inactions. That's not a weak or blind acceptance of our circumstances in the face of a bigger, stronger God who tramples all over us in the process, but an acknowledgement of the fact that His wisdom and authority are beyond our understanding because His ways are not our ways (Isa. 55:8).

We cannot see the heavenly flip side of His earthly plan for us. What we do know is that God never condemns us and is always working for our good (Rom. 8:28).

IN PRACTICE

A PATHWAY TO PEACE

If we are trying to help someone who is angry with God – perhaps they are grieving a loss – our role is to facilitate them to come to a place of acceptance and recognition of who God is and what that means for their future beyond a healthy expression of anger. Coming to that place means being led along a specific pathway:

1. Acknowledging that it's OK to be honest and angry before God.
2. Knowing that neither God nor we condemn them for their anger.
3. Offering to stand with them in their anger, sharing the pain and bearing the blast.

(This early part of the pathway takes time, needs space and often requires our companionship as a multitude of anger-rooted emotions are expressed.)

4. Helping them to 'cut the anger down to size' by gaining a better perspective on it.
5. Finding the means to help them express their anger to God: through drawing, writing an 'angry' psalm or letter and destroying it or surrendering it to God in some way – perhaps during a Communion service.

   (It's important that we understand the person we are trying to help in order to find the way of expression that is most helpful to them.)
6. And, lastly, we bring hope. The Bible clearly tells us that God can use even the most painful experiences for good and can turn them round: the cross being the ultimate example. We may know pain – but beyond that pain there is resurrection to come. That gives us hope.

Sue and Max's story

Hope is perhaps the most transforming thing we can offer in the face of pain, bewilderment and anger.

In a split second one July day, Max Sinclair's life was dramatically changed. His neck was broken in a car accident. Evangelist, father of three, optimistic for the future, he suddenly faced the terrible possibility of permanent paralysis. Hundreds prayed. Hopes for recovery were raised, dashed and finally miraculously realised when Max became only the fourth patient to walk out of the spinal injuries unit in Stoke Mandeville Hospital in twenty years.

Max's story tells how, as he made a slow and agonising recovery, he and his wife Sue learned about anger and suffering in the most surprising ways:

… Sue burst into the ward more excitedly than usual and held a posy of tiny wild flowers over my head.

'Look Mac, aren't these lovely?' Bright red and yellow vetch peeped through fronds of grasses, together with daisies and soft purple campion. Globes of dandelion too, and more purple flowers I didn't recognise.

'Where did you find those?' I asked …

'Just outside.' Sue was breathless and her eyes shone. 'They were growing on a *rubbish dump*!'

'Really?' Susie was capable of finding something pretty in the most obscure places.

'I walk past it every day – it belongs to the hospital, I think. I never noticed all these lovely flowers before, though. Who'd have thought a rubbish dump could be anything but ugly and useless …

'They looked so odd, in among the broken bottles and bits of paper … you should have seen how they clung to the tiniest bits of soil …

'You know, I had an idea, while I was looking at those flowers on the rubbish dump … what's happened to you, to us … 'Another pause.

'It's like the rubbish dump in a way. I mean …' She frowned, as if the words had already come out wrongly. 'I mean, your suffering and paralysis seem awful, pointless, a waste of your life. Yet we don't know what God might do with our life as it is now. To him it isn't a waste. If he can bring flowers from that heap of rubbish, what might he bring out of our situation?'

'You mean God doesn't take away things that are difficult, painful, but transforms them – brings something else from them, like the flowers? Well, I wonder what flowers he'll grow on our rubbish dump?'[5]

ACTIVITY

Look back to one particular part of this chapter which has special relevance for you in a situation of anger. (It will very likely be the part with which you have had –ironically – some argument or during which you felt uncomfortable!) How might you use what you have read to address your issues of anger before God?

Use your notebook to focus on a particular area of anger in your life. Now write down:

What was *done* or *said* to cause that anger;
How you are *feeling* about it;
What you are *thinking* about it:
What you *believe* about that anger:
How your *mood* relates to and stimulates that anger.

REFLECTION

Now consider whether you have made any errors in your thinking which have impacted your beliefs and left you feeling angry.

Bring your angry thoughts, beliefs and feelings before God and ask Him to help you discern truth from fiction, honesty from self-deception and to recognise the need for perspective and forgiveness rather than blame or bitterness.

PRAYER

'Search me O God, and know my heart;
    test me and know my anxious thoughts.
See if there is any offensive way in me,
    and lead me in the way everlasting.'

                    Psalm 139:23–24

(You may like to use the whole of Psalm 139 as a prayer.)

CHAPTER 4

A PRACTICAL APPROACH IN HANDLING ANGER

INTRODUCTION

We have discovered that anger is an emotion which affects the body as much as the mind. Its physical effects can be damaging not only in terms of our own health and safety but the health and safety of others too. Understanding the impact that physical anger has on each of us and how we might control those physical manifestations can take us some way towards managing it effectively.

The final part of this book concentrates in some detail on the practical ways in which we might handle anger – both our own and the anger of other people when directed towards us.

It suggests skills we might develop, outlines priorities for daily life and offers practical anger management techniques to help us deal with anger 'as it happens'.

MANAGING THE BODY'S REACTION TO ANGER

There are three ways in which we can help ourselves – and each other – to manage anger physiologically. By:

1. Learning the value and techniques of deep breathing.
2. Understanding the benefit of regular relaxation.
3. Prioritising a balanced lifestyle.

1. Learning the value and techniques of deep breathing

Slow, controlled breathing is used as an aid to relaxation. If we can catch the anger by *breathing* ourselves calm, we can approach the issues related to our anger in a calmer way, and deal with them with a clearer head.

Therefore if we can identify our rising anger right at the outset – before it has donned its boxing gloves and armour – the result of 'breathing ourselves calm' can be very powerful because it helps us to simmer down. However, if we can't catch our anger at the outset, moving to another room as the anger 'bites', and following through the breathing exercise, will slow down our reactions and calm our anger.

Once our anger has gone beyond a certain point and is exploding we will need to deal with it differently. (Note: First Aid action, page 105.)

IN PRACTICE

BREATHING OURSELVES CALM

- First, sit down in a comfortable chair.
- Be aware of the chair taking your weight, and become responsive to how still you are. Are you are hearing noises around or listening to thoughts?
- Try putting your thoughts in an imaginary box and place that box on an imaginary shelf. Think of peace and calm.
- Be aware of your breathing and try to slow it down. Breathe in and out through your nose.
- Note which breath is easier to make, the in-breath (inhalation) or the out-breath (exhalation).
- Now count how long your in-breath takes and how long your out-breath takes.
- Carry on breathing to identify this rhythm.
- Now make the out-breath longer than the in-breath. For example, if the in-breath is three counts long, make the out-breath five counts long (2/5 ... or 4/6, 5/8, etc).
- Every time you breathe out, do it slowly with a sigh, rather like a balloon deflating. Continue for a few more minutes to breathe deeply and relax.
- Note how much more relaxed your body is.

(It's important to make the out-breaths longer than the in-breaths because this dampens down the arousal response.)

- Practise breathing using this technique for a few minutes daily and use it when you begin to feel uptight with anger.

2. Understanding the benefit of regular relaxation

Often the first thing we are aware of when we notice an anger trigger is physical tension – a hunching of shoulders, clenching of fists and/or a stiffness in our body position. It follows, then, that if we are able to relax our bodies we will begin to defuse some of the tension and dispel at least some of the anger.

If we are chronically angry, that tension may be a permanent fixture, manifesting itself in various physical symptoms and illnesses. We may also be exhausted by 'holding ourselves together'.

Every one of us has our own unique way of relaxing: curling up with a good book; taking the dog for a walk; listening to music; enjoying a long hot bubble bath.

Making relaxation a regular part of our lives (see point 3 on page 90) will enable us to make better use of it in response to anger, and will keep our base levels of stress and tension down.

IN PRACTICE

LEARNING TO RELAX

- Choose at least two activities which enable you to relax completely and 'shut out the world'. Endeavour to fit them into your schedule on a regular basis.
- When you feel yourself beginning to get angry, imagine yourself in that place of relaxation. If possible – even if at a later time – return to that place to reinforce your mental image and 'relax' your anger.
- Practise the following relaxation exercise:

RELAXATION EXERCISE

- Sit or lie as comfortably as possible and close your eyes. (If as you do this exercise you experience unusual sensations such as tingling or light-headedness, it is quite normal. If you open your eyes they will go away, and as you carry on with the exercise the feelings will disappear.)
- Become aware of your breathing.
- Keeping your eyelids closed, screw your eyes up tight and relax.
- Notice the tiredness in those muscles around your eyes.
- Let the warmth of God's healing light relax those muscles further.
- Let that feeling of warmth travel to every part of your face, jaw, tongue, neck. Relax and bathe in God's healing light.
- Concentrate on your breathing.
- Then let the healing warmth travel slowly down through every part of your body, stopping regularly to pause and concentrate on your breathing.
- Allow the healing warmth to relax your shoulders, to travel down your right arm, down through the muscles, down to your fingertips. Do the same with the left arm. Let the relaxation travel down to your chest; your back; and down each leg in turn.
- Pause for a few moments.
- Go back and concentrate on any part of the body you would like to relax further.
- Now concentrate on your favourite relaxing place (real or imagined). Try and see it in your mind's eye. Identify the shapes and colours, the sounds, the smells.

- Imagine touching something in this peaceful place.
- Is Jesus in this place? Is He saying anything to you?
- Feel more and more relaxed.
- Stay in this place of peace and relaxation until you are ready to return to the room, taking your own time to do this slowly.

3. Prioritising a balanced lifestyle

'All work and no play makes Jack a dull boy' we are proverbially told, but it may also make him an angry one.

Carl Jung said, 'Hurry is not just of the devil – it *is* the devil.' Most of us need to make a concerted effort to eliminate hurry from our lives, to take time out to reflect and to gain a sense of perspective. That means marking out time for relaxation and play alongside our busy working, family and church lives – and protecting that time keenly. It is ironic that in the Christian community, Sunday – the day of rest – is often the busiest!

In a busy week, we often make the excuse that we haven't got time to stop or slow down. But if we do, we often find that the time spent slowing helps us to return to work with a refreshed body, a sharper mind, a renewed passion – and maybe a few creative ideas which 'slow' has brought to fruition, or which would otherwise have been missed in the rush.

Achieving a lifestyle which includes a balance of silence, company, relaxation, rest, busyness, sociability, challenge and creativity will help keep our mood on an even keel. It will mean that we will meet any potential for anger from a place of optimum emotional and physical health and be better equipped to deal with it in a healthy way.

IN PRACTICE

PRIORITISING A BALANCED LIFESTYLE

- Make windows in your diary at intervals when you will take time out - an hour once a day, a half day once a week, a day once a fortnight and a week once a quarter should be the *minimum* to aim for.
- Remember that relaxation is a priority - not an 'If I get time' add-on.
- Occasionally check the balance of your diary: Ask yourself how much work, play, exercise, relaxation, time for friends and family and time for solitude is listed and consider redressing the balance: this is a matter of life and health.
- Review your diet and exercise priorities - how much do they suggest a balanced lifestyle?

MANAGING THE THOUGHTS THAT FEED OUR ANGER

Our thoughts feed our anger. They justify it, encourage it and give reasons for maintaining it. But in the midst of anger those thoughts are often unreliable, untruthful and damaging.

In order to handle our anger well it is important that we learn to identify, challenge and, if necessary, change any unrealistic, irrational or untrue thoughts presented to us by our anger.

IDENTIFYING AND CHANGING UNREALISTIC AND IRRATIONAL THOUGHTS

Challenging and changing the unrealistic thoughts that feed our anger is a matter of *choice*.

We must choose to...

- Acknowledge and evaluate thoughts that accompany angry feelings.

By ...

Asking ourselves: Is that true? Did that really happen? Did she really say that? Is that my assumption or a reality? Why am I angry? What does this anger mean? Where does it come from?

- Identify and challenge rigid beliefs labelled 'should', 'must', 'ought' that arise in the midst of anger.

Instead of saying, 'He should have done that'– a rigid demand – choose to say, 'I wish he hadn't done that' – a flexible request, removing the emotive outcome.

Ask, 'What is the origin of my "ought", "must" and "should"? Who says?'

- Replace old irrational self-talk with new rational self-talk in reaction to anger.

Instead of 'I hate myself, and losing my temper just goes to show that I am not a nice person', say, 'I recognise that I am a fallible human being who is trying to learn how to handle anger more appropriately. God recognises my sinful nature and still loves me, so I will work on accepting and loving myself.'

This may take longer and require some concentrated effort – but we're worth it!

• Replace lies with God's truth.

Ask: 'Is that really the case – or am I adding some evidence to weight my argument?'

• Become aware of displaced anger.

Ask: 'Am I angry with this person – or are they a scapegoat?' 'Where might my anger be appropriately placed?' 'Why do I find it difficult to express that anger appropriately?' 'How can I learn to do so?'

• Remind ourselves that God is in control.

Examining our anger before God often means borrowing His 'lens' in order to see our anger for what it is.

Sometimes all we can do is hand that anger over to Him in surrender, trusting Him for its resolution and reminding ourselves that whatever we *feel* and whatever happens, He is in control. Surrendering anger may be something we have to repeat again and again (we are good at taking it back!) but we can know real release if we do so with a sincere heart.

'ON THE SPOT' ANGER MANAGEMENT
The above tactics may take time and reflection as part of a longer process of anger management.

But what if we need help RIGHT NOW!?

PRACTICAL 'ON THE SPOT' STRATEGIES
For most of us, the majority of our anger will be in response to

day-to-day stresses and strains, confrontation and disagreement. Anger is a practical occurrence that needs practical responses. How, where and when we face anger will dictate how we deal with it.

Joe Griffin says, 'Anger is a gift from nature, anger can initiate change, but shouldn't control our reaction to it. It's about learning strategies to help us.'

It can help to tuck some practical ideas under our belt in advance for dealing with angry thoughts 'On the Spot'.

IN PRACTICE

TEN-SECOND ANGER DELAY

At the first sign of anger, immediately engage the rational brain. Experiment to see what works for you: identify different colours around you; words beginning with the same letter; counting backwards from one hundred in threes, etc. This buys you the ten to twelve seconds needed to subvert the otherwise imminent emotional hijack.

STANDING BACK

Sometimes, we need to learn to stand back to look at the 'scene' we are part of. In other words, to *avoid* an explosion – DON'T light the blue touchpaper – but stand well back! To 'stand back' in a potentially explosive situation try:

1. The 'friend technique'

Ask: 'How would an all-knowing, all-wise friend advise me to view this situation?'

2. Reframing the situation

Where are the good aspects of this situation? Find five ways to look at the situation positively.

(Sometimes it can help to jot down those five positive views of a long-term situation and keep them nearby, in your bag or in a safe and private place on your desk as a frequent reminder.)

3. Conducting a cost-benefit analysis

Become an anger accountant! Examine the costs and benefits of your current system of appraisal (costs and benefits to the situation, the people involved, your emotional tank, the stability of the current situation, future fall-out) and then look for a more 'cost-effective' way to deal with it.

4. Having time out to cool down

If someone else is involved in your anger, agree a time to sit down with them at a later date to talk about the issues: a time when you have both had an opportunity to think through the issues calmly and logically from all angles.

Do NOT view this interim as time out to build your case!

If it's a situation that is angering you alone and you want to understand and deal with that anger, make an appointment with yourself and the anger when you have calmed down and make an effort to work through the issues. You may need a pen and paper, or a wise and patient friend who will help you to look at the details from a fresh perspective with a view to resolution – not justification!

IN PRACTICE

LEARN HOW TO HANDLE ANGER: A PRACTICAL MODEL

L – Listening, rather than jumping to conclusions:
- getting more information before responding
- listening to your own feelings and what your body is saying

E – Every situation demands a choice – I choose to become angry.

A – Acknowledging weaknesses in yourself and others.

R – Responding rather than reacting:
- learning to relax (count one to ten)
- carrying out cost/benefit analysis
- identifying and expressing the feeling beneath the anger ('I feel hurt and angry when ...')
- challenging irrational self-talk

N – Never losing sight of God.

THE 3Rs APPROACH TO HANDLING ESCALATING ANGER (RELAX, REFLECT, RESPOND)

1. Take note of any trigger and stop what you are doing.
2. Check your body – what is it telling you?

3. Release your physical tension – physical exercise, breathing and/or relaxation exercises.
4. Analyse what is going on:

Ask:
- Does this situation remind me of any other? Has an old wound been opened?
- Do I feel threatened? If so, do I perceive this rationally or am I exaggerating it?
- Am I projecting a feeling or quality into the situation which actually belongs to me?
- Am I under stress?
- Am I taking responsibility for my own behaviour?

5. Don't put off expressing how you feel for long periods and withdraw into silence.
6. Write or mentally compose a new script. If someone else is involved, carefully prepare your words to open up a discussion which hopefully will lead to some resolution, or at the very least, inform the other person of your feelings.

HANDLING ANGER AND RESENTMENT GOD'S WAY

We all experience situations that cause the kind of misunderstanding that leads to anger and resentment. We are flawed, sensitive human beings and will inevitably experience times when we are hurt by others of the same variety!

How we cope with that hurt will depend on our self-esteem, our level of anxiety, related anger and any deep resentment that might be within us. Jesus tells us to forgive a multitude of times – seventy-seven times seven, in fact (Matt. 18:22) and to forgive because we are first forgiven (Col. 3:13) by God, who says 'For I will forgive their wickedness and will remember their sins no more' (Jer. 31:34). God will not judge us on those forgiven sins. He will let them go – as far as the east is from the west (Psa. 103:12) and will not remember them.

It's important, therefore, that we don't hold judgment against anybody else. Harbouring resentment leads to unforgiveness and a slow bitterness that will inevitably infect all of our being.

There is no alternative – we need to learn to forgive.

THE IMPORTANCE OF FORGIVENESS

Forgiveness is the key to leaving pain and anger behind and moving on. Ironically, the act of forgiving is often harder to anticipate than to actually do. Yet, forgiveness is still costly because it is about each of us surrendering our rights: the right to 'hurt you back if you hurt me'.

WHAT IS FORGIVENESS?

In *The Freedom of Forgiveness*, David Augsberger writes, 'The man who forgives pays a tremendous price – the price of the evil he forgives! ... If I break a priceless heirloom that you treasure and you forgive me, you bear the loss and I go free.'[1]

Jay Adams suggests that forgiveness between 'friends' is not a feeling, but a commitment or promise to three things:

- 'I will not use it against my friend in the future.'
- 'I will not talk to others about my friend.'
- 'I will not dwell on it myself.'[2]

Adams suggests that 'God hasn't given you the authority (the right) to take vengeance. ("Revenge is mine, I will repay," says the Lord.' Rom 12:19) God hasn't given you the ability to take any form of reprisal. Nor has God not given you the knowledge of what is truly fair.'[3]

The goal of forgiveness is restoration and reconciliation of relationship.

If bitterness and revenge are present, then forgiveness is not. Revenge lowers us to our enemy's level – forgiveness elevates us above it.

Mark Twain said, 'Forgiveness is the fragrance the violet sheds on the heel that has crushed it.'

These are fine words and principles regarding forgiveness. Although forgiving someone can seem such a mountainous task, we often fail to see the relative simplicity of forgiveness from the depths of our pain. We say, 'I can't forgive them. I won't.' Or, in reality, 'I don't want to.' It may be difficult even to be willing to pray that God will change our heart. But to do so is obedience to His command that we forgive one another. He knows how hard it is for us but He will lead us step by step and work with us to change heart and mind and action if our desire is to obey Him.

He can – and will – enable us to live in the light of His forgiveness and our forgiveness of others.

Often those who have hurt us will not even know that they have done so, because they may have acted in innocence or ignorance. The result may be that we have carried our hurt around without confrontation for some time and will still need to forgive them, sometimes many years later.

It may help to remember Jesus' words from the cross, where our forgiveness was established: 'Father, forgive them, for they do not know what they are doing' (Luke 23:34).

Forgiveness may be a powerful witness to those who have lived with anger, fear and unforgiveness, or who are intent on revenge.

Wendy attended the thanksgiving service of the eighteen-year-old son of Christian friends. Sam[4] had died as a result of an incident on a summer afternoon in a West Country seaside resort. Jumped upon by two men who had something against him, he was fatally beaten and died later in hospital from multiple head injuries.

The group of young men of which Sam had been part were a close and affectionate crowd. Many had experienced great difficulties and challenges in their young lives, but they had learnt to support, encourage and care for one another. As far as was known, none – apart from Sam – had known a Christian background or upbringing or had come to faith.

Sam's thanksgiving service was a moving, loving and poignant celebration of a young life not without its own difficulties. Sam's mum and dad told how they had worked through many problems with Sam in his teenage years – and how others had been beyond all of them. They delighted in the fact that in the year or so before his death there had been a renewed closeness, maturity and sense of responsibility in Sam and that their relationship was better than it had ever been.

Instead of voicing their anger at his untimely death, Sam's parents shared their pain with honesty; instead of laying blame, they asked for forgiveness and understanding.

The effect of such a gentle and grace-filled message on the other members of Sam's group was clear. They had, quite literally, never heard anything like it. They were stunned, quietened and visibly moved by the words they heard and the attitude they witnessed.

Instead of the revenge they sought, they were asked to consider grace, peace and forgiveness. No act of retaliation, they were told, would ever bring Sam back. This was the better way.[5]

HOW TO DEAL WITH A BACKLOG OF UNRESOLVED ANGER

Sometimes we can carry unresolved anger with us for such a long time and in such a deep place, that it almost becomes a trait of our personality and a regular part of our daily lives. It may seem hidden, but it will make itself known when we least expect it: often when a similar emotion in the present reminds us of the past. We find we cannot have a feeling today which is disconnected from similar feelings yesterday.

We cannot change the past, but we can change the way we feel about it. Holding in a backlog of unacknowledged or unexpressed anger is potentially self-destructive and harmful to others.

God desires truth in our inner parts (Psa. 51:6). There is a link between truth and honesty and emotional health. In order to experience emotional, mental and spiritual health, it is important that we honestly face our anger and work through it.

When we hold on tightly to unresolved anger issues from the past, we will feel them again as they arise as if for the first time. Our stomach will churn and our memories return. It is important to bring those feelings to God in prayer – to be honest with Him about them rather than burying them again.

If we are to move on beyond our anger – even if it is only much later that we acknowledge that we have done so – we need to accept it, process it, ask for forgiveness, forgive in turn and *move on*.

Recently, a burst pipe made a hole in the road outside Wendy's house. For some time the water belched through the crack, making the hole larger and the surface uneven. The road was closed and it was several days before anyone could drive along it.

When the workmen came to repair the hole, residents were fascinated by their approach. In order to repair the pipe and the hole, the workmen had to dig much deeper and wider than the hole made by the original burst. They checked the pipe along the whole of its exposed length, and mended it to prevent any more leaks. Then they filled the hole to the surface once more, ensuring that the same problem would be unlikely to occur again. The road could then be opened and traffic flowed once more, driving over the scar which clearly showed the repaired – but now entirely sound – patch.

We need to check our anger at source, do all we can to make sure it won't burst again, mend the damage it has caused as far as we are able – and move on. We may 'drive over' the repaired patch – the scar – on a daily basis, but we will not feel a need to dig it up again or risk it erupting into our lives. In time, our scar – like that patch of repaired road – will be barely recognisable.

IN PRACTICE

LETTING GO OF ANGER – A PRACTICAL RESPONSE

It is vital that all the energy associated with anger is dealt with and let go.

How we deal with and release that anger will depend on our circumstances and our personality.

We might consider:

- Writing a 'not to be posted' letter to the person who has hurt us and caused the anger. We allow the letter to flow from the heart, releasing the pain, and using whatever angry words feel most expressive and which are as direct and specific regarding events, words, and incidents as possible. We should NEVER send the letter, however tempted we may feel.
- Drawing or painting a picture of our anger, using figures or symbols.
- Making a confidential tape recording in which we pour out our heart.

Then we bring our words or pictures before God in prayer, ask for forgiveness and acknowledge our forgiveness of the other person.

The letters, pictures tapes or CDs may then be torn up, shredded or safely burned.

(As suggested earlier, we might ask the permission of our minister or church leader to place this package of words on the Communion table in a private Communion service, symbolising the release of the anger and allowing God to carry it.)

Sometimes it may be helpful to keep these items in a safe place to look back on at a later date in recognition and acceptance – even joy – at the forgiveness given. But it may not be wise for us to keep these records if they could be vulnerable to other prying eyes, or we believe that re-reading or reconsidering their contents may only rekindle our anger.

• Finally, acknowledge and accept – before God and/or in the confidence of a trusted Christian friend – that your anger, like your words/pictures, has been dealt with.

THE IMPORTANCE OF WORDS

Sometimes our words really can make all the difference – they can act as balm or bomb! Before we spend time with the person we are angry with – or who is angry with us – we may simply need to stop and think about what to say, and what not to say.

RESOLVING ANGER WITH ANOTHER PERSON THROUGH DISCUSSION

We must:

- Acknowledge and take responsibility for our anger.
- Be as objective as we can in stating our complaint.
- Have a humble heart and be open to criticism.
- Address one issue at a time.
- Talk about our anger in private, not in the public domain.
- Always use the 'I' word rather than use the 'you' word. ('I feel' rather than 'you do'.)
- Start with something positive, not negative: 'I value our relationship so I want to clear the air.'
- Be specific and don't over-generalise: 'You always …'
- Not accuse others of making us angry: 'I get angry when …'

rather than 'you make me angry'.
- Not put ourselves down with self-deprecating self-talk.
- Not lay ourselves open for retaliatory anger: 'I know that I'm forgetful … but don't shout at me when I tell you I have forgotten …'
- Not bring up past grievances (historical anger!).
- Not label, mind-read, preach or moralise.
- Not criticise or attack the *person*; focus our words on their behaviour.
- Not make idle threats.
- Try to find a way that both parties' needs are met.

And finally …

- Remember that anger resolution is not about winning or losing – but resolving.

But what do we do when there is no question of talking – because everything happens too fast and too furiously? How do we handle explosive anger?

IN PRACTICE

HANDLING EXPLOSIVE ANGER – FIRST AID ACTION
1. *Withdraw* from the situation and calm down. (It can take twenty minutes for the body to calm down fully.)
2. *During time out*, don't spend time rehearsing the grievances because that will keep the physiological arousal going, so do something that is distracting and relaxing:

- Physical – sport, a walk, housework, a swim
- Mental – a crossword, Sudoku, reading
- Breathing or relaxation exercises – see pages 88 and 89.

HOW TO HANDLE ANOTHER'S DANGEROUSLY EXPLOSIVE ANGER

Goal – to postpone any (negative) resolution of the conflict.

Action:
- Keep cool and calm.
- Positive internal self-talk.
- Speak slowly with eye contact, indicating you are listening.
- Share your own feelings and fears.
- Check the position of your body – and theirs: What does it say? What might it do?
- In a dangerous situation, keep your eyes open for something to throw – not to throw *at* the person, but something that could be safely thrown to make a noise hopefully to distract the person from their anger.
- If things look as if they will get out of control, ie physical aggression, extricate self from situation – gradually move towards door or other safe exit route; or, if possible and practicable without furthering the aggression, find a means to summon help.

ROAD RAGE

So-called 'road rage' is a newly defined form of anger. It first entered the *Oxford English Dictionary* in 1997 as a term used to describe our reaction to those we feel are unfit to travel on the roads.

Environmental and sociological reasons for road rage:

- More traffic increases a driver's level of frustration. (A blocked goal!)
- A faster pace of life demands a frequent need to make instant reactions, putting the body in a high arousal state.
- People enraged on the roads often see drivers and passengers as objects rather than people.

Psychological reasons:

- The increased time pressure on individuals.
- In viewing self as 'No. 1', we demonise other drivers.
- We don't know them so it's 'not personal'.

IN PRACTICE

AVOIDING ROAD RAGE
Dealing with road rage in others needs tactics in line with 'dealing with explosive anger'.

Our own road rage needs the following:

- Monitoring of our own physiological state.
  We need to try to calm ourselves down when arousal is high. (Deep breathe; sing; smile at the person in the car next to us – and at ourselves in the mirror! Play calm music in the car; stop in a lay-by and pray!; stop to take a look at a beautiful view and take stock; if appropriate, break our journey for a coffee and a rest.)

- Changing of self-talk.
- We need to attempt to change our self-talk. 'How much will this matter tomorrow?', 'Is it really that bad?', 'Why not be the calmest person on the road today?', 'Just how calm can I be?', 'She's a motorist – not a monster'.

- Reframing of what is going on.
  Reframing doesn't have to be true, but it should enable a positive – even comical – response. 'If I don't yell (or yell back) at this man, he will do all my ironing for the next month(!)' (We will have to deal with the anger resulting from the fact that he doesn't, later!)

Research shows that the most potent ingredient is helping the other person – or ourselves – to gain a new perspective on the problem:

'The heat/rain/snow/football results/234 shopping days till Christmas are making us all grouchy today, aren't they?'

Tactics aren't everything, and we will often struggle to remember them as we feel the anger rising! But a few tactics remembered and practised until they become habits can make a considerable difference – to our anger, our heart rate, our stress level – and those fast-encroaching forehead lines!

Our first 'tactic' as Christians faced with anger is, of course, prayer: instant, always accessible and infinitely powerful. A prayer sent heavenward the moment we feel an angry response is a request for: an instantaneous spiritual anger audit; the resources of heaven to cope with anger; and the wisdom of the Holy Spirit to have insight, understanding and a spirit of peace and forgiveness. It is up to us to pray first – point the finger (if at all) second.

ACTIVITY
Which of the 'In practice' suggestions can you resolve to learn, practise and make a habit over the next few weeks?

How will you remind yourself to do so?

REFLECTION
Read the story of Jesus before His accusers and Pilate from Matthew 26:47–68; Mark 15:1–20; Luke 22:47–52 or John 19.

What does the example of Jesus teach us about anger – and our behaviour in the face of anger?

PRAYER
Lord, in the face of anger, or when anger is in my face, let me turn it first to You.

CONCLUSION

PUTTING IT ALL INTO PRACTICE: LIVING POSITIVELY WITH ANGER

Anger is a fact of life – but it is also a gift from God. Anger can initiate change but it shouldn't control our reaction to change. Living with anger in an effective and healthy way is about learning strategies to help control angry feelings and understanding and resolving the causes of them.

Many of us find that our concerns about our anger add guilt, remorse, regret and feelings of inadequacy and helplessness to an already difficult load.

But we need not live this way.

There is a way through with our own commitment, care from others and in the love, forgiveness and grace of God.

For many of us, learning to approach anger in a healthy way will resemble a slow plod on a difficult road. Often we will feel we have made ten steps forward only to make five back. The

111

road to managing anger is not an easy one but it takes us on a journey worth making. It's a journey God will take alongside us. He knows what it is to be angry; our anger doesn't frighten or surprise Him: 'He can take it – His shoulders are broad enough.'

EXTENDED ACTIVITY

Thinking ahead about how we might apply various strategies for anger management may help us – and help us to help others – to respond to anger positively.

The following scenarios might be resolved in the light of what has been understood in Chapters One to Three of this book and using one or more of the strategies we considered in Chapter Four. Using what you have learned – how would you respond to each?

1. Eric often feels angry with his young teenage son. Eric says he had discovered that his son had been lying to him about his smoking habit, saying that he didn't smoke, but Eric could smell it on his breath. This led Eric to impulsively hit his son across the face and send him to his room. Eric asked his son to forgive him, but his son refused to speak to him for days. Eric says that he sometimes takes this habitual untruthfulness in his stride, and other times because he has had a stressful, exhausting day at work, he takes it out on his son. He also thinks there are times when he is just in a bad mood. However, he is very worried about the effect he is having on his son in trying to deal with his lies – particularly considering his role model as a Christian father.

Which of the following strategies would you consider to help Eric and his son?

- Find ways to remove the trigger for anger. How might you help Eric to do that?
- Encourage him to consider changing the evaluation and judgment of the situation so that he sees it in a different way. How might he change his perspective?
- Tackle the fact that Eric is not dealing with his anger appropriately, eg ask if he is displacing it on someone else? Or suppressing it?
- Help Eric to alter the response to the situation by considering a strategy to change behaviour that follows a trigger. What would you suggest?
- Identify and change any irrational beliefs that may be feeding his anger. How would that process be managed?
- Identify unmet needs, blocked goals, any faulty concept of God, and help Eric understand how to meet needs in God. Who might help him to do that?
- What is contributing to Eric's mood changes? What can be changed? How? What kind of ongoing support will he need?

2. Tom and Susy are both well-known church leaders. Tom sometimes gets very angry with Susy because she says things about their private life which he views as best left unsaid in public. Which of the strategies above would you consider?

3. Bonny, aged eighteen years, sometimes gets very depressed, irritable and angry with her family because of 'boyfriend trouble'. She longs to have a long-term partner, but only has occasional boyfriends. This upsets her, and she takes it out on her family: they see her as a moody and very angry young lady. She is also angry with God and doesn't go to church any

more. Her anger is gradually driving away many of her friends. Which of the strategies would you consider?

4. Mike gets really angry with his partner, hitting out at her when she doesn't do what he asks her to do. He recognises that he is a 'control freak' and wants to control her. He feels his anger is uncontrollable at times and is concerned about this as he fears he may seriously hurt her, albeit unintentionally. Although he recognises he is a bully at work, he is comfortable about this, as work is going well and he has been particularly successful – in fact he is a millionaire. He is also particularly angry when he returns from visiting his mother, but doesn't know why. Which of the previous strategies would you consider?

5. Elaine describes herself as 'stressed out'. She has a high-powered job, and more work than she can cope with; she has two children (eight and ten years) and a husband who is away on business a lot. She feels guilty when she 'snaps' at the children and feels an utter failure as a mum because of this. Feeling very lonely in her marriage, she often goes into quiet moods even when her husband is around. She says she wants to change. Which of the strategies would you consider?

EXTENDED REFLECTION

Many of us will want to make our focus on anger management a biblical one – we have already mentioned something of what the Bible has to say about anger.

The Psalms – especially the psalms of David – model a human response to anger well: Psalm 28 is typical of that model. The extended reflection which follows uses Psalm 28 as a model for handling anger. It may not dot all the i's and cross all the t's where anger is concerned – but it gives us a helpful framework for dealing biblically and simply with our own anger before God.

PSALM 28: A BIBLICAL MODEL FOR LIVING POSITIVELY WITH ANGER

To you I call, O LORD my Rock;
　　do not turn a deaf ear to me.
For if you remain silent,
　　I shall be like those who have gone down to the pit.
Hear my cry for mercy
　　as I call to you for help,
as I lift up my hands
　　towards your Most Holy Place.

Do not drag me away with the wicked,
　　with those who do evil,
who speak cordially with their neighbours
　　but harbour malice in their hearts.
Repay them for their deeds
　　and for their evil work;
repay them for what their hands have done
　　and bring back upon them what they deserve.
Since they show no regard for the works of the LORD
　　and what his hands have done,
he will tear them down
　　and never build them up again.

Praise be to the LORD,
　　for he has heard my cry for mercy.
The LORD is my strength and my shield;

my heart trusts in him, and I am helped.
My heart leaps for joy
    and I will give thanks to him in song.

The LORD is the strength of his people,
    a fortress of salvation for his anointed one.
Save your people and bless your inheritance;
    be their shepherd and carry them for ever.

David vents his anger to God in all the ways we might do.

Look at verses 1–2: 'I call'; '[I] cry' 'I lift up my hands'. Lifting up hands was the traditional way for David and his contemporaries to pray. He was able to almost literally lift his anger to God in prayer.

- How might different modes of expression and physical actions help us express our anger to God honestly?

In verses 3–5, David is almost viciously honest. He tells God in no uncertain terms what he wants to see happen! There is much detail, pain, hurt, resentment and disappointment in these verses. Most of all there is *honesty*. David is real before God.

- What do David's words tell us about the first – and safest – place to take our hurt and angry feelings?

Nothing has changed between verses 1–5 and verse 6 – except David himself!

Having offloaded all of his anger and anxiety onto God, he is left with God alone as his focus. David's heart is turned towards the God who has accepted his anger and honesty: in verses 6–7 his heart is turned to praise.

- What part might praise and worship have in the process of our dealing with anger?

The final verses – 7–9 – see David reminding himself of the characteristics of God as One who can be trusted: 'strength'; 'fortress'; saviour and 'shepherd'. It is God who matters now – not David's pile of angry grievances. He has regained his bearings and his focus. It is as if David is saying that God is bigger than all his complaints and all of his anger.

- How might reminding ourselves of the unchanging nature and character of God help us deal with our anger?

PRAYER

Heavenly Father, You know what it is to be angry; to forgive; to weep; to be betrayed; to be isolated. There is not one tiny sensation of human experience that You do not understand fully.

Therefore, we can bring our burden of anger before You, even as we stagger under its weight. And we can leave it with You, at the foot of the cross where Your Son cried out to save us from ourselves.

Thank You, Father, for Your forgiveness, Your love, Your grace, Your mercy and Your justice.

Hold us in Your arms, Lord.

Amen.

GOD IS BIGGER THAN OUR ANGER

Throughout the writing of this book, a clear picture has unintentionally emerged. You may have noticed it as you have read – a recurring theme of the arms of God.

I believe that God is asking us to carry our anger to the safety of His strong, eternal and loving arms. Only there, in a place of acceptance, peace and forgiveness can we know a release from our anger in the security of His wisdom and understanding.

Like a little child in a tantrum, God enfolds us in His lap, reassuring us, calming our fury, crushing it with his love and stilling our raging hearts.

From that safe place, we realise that God is so much bigger than our anger – and that He is all that matters.

Wendy Bray

APPENDIX

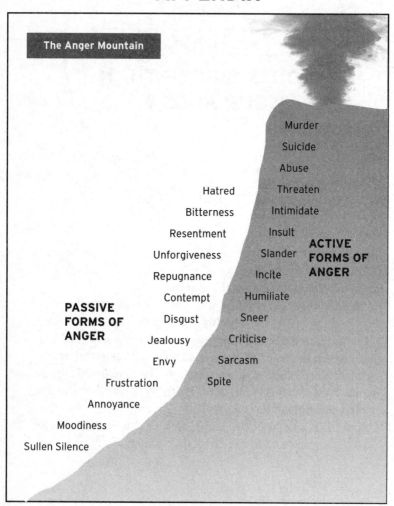

The Anger Mountain

Murder
Suicide
Abuse
Threaten
Intimidate
Insult
Slander
Incite
Humiliate
Sneer
Criticise
Sarcasm
Spite

ACTIVE FORMS OF ANGER

Hatred
Bitterness
Resentment
Unforgiveness
Repugnance
Contempt
Disgust
Jealousy
Envy
Frustration
Annoyance
Moodiness
Sullen Silence

PASSIVE FORMS OF ANGER

NOTES

CHAPTER 1

1. *Penguin English Dictionary* (London: Penguin, 2000), p.48.
2. BBC News, Sunday 6 June 2004.
3. BBC News, Wednesday 26 May 2004.
4. BBC Health, October 2000 (from www.bbc.co.uk/health).
5. Crime in England and Wales 2004/5 report, The Home Office.
6. RAC Foundation www.racfoundation.org.uk
7. *Daily Mail*, 26 September 2006.
8. E.L. Rossi, *The Psychobiology of Mind-Body Healing* (NY: W.W. Norton & Co. Ltd., New Ed. Edition, 1989), also Rossi *The 20 Minute Break* (Phoenix, AZ: Zeig, Tucker & Co., Inc., 1991).
9. C. Tavris, *Anger: The Misunderstood Emotion* (London: Simon & Schuster, 1982).
10. See www.nursingresearchonline.com
11. *The Times*, 22 April 2006.
12. Joe Griffin with Ivan Tyrrell, *Effective Anger Management* (East Sussex: Piers Bishop, 2002). Also available as a CD.
13. See www.nursingresearchonline.com
14. Matthew Ostow's quote from Tim LaHaye, *Anger is a Choice* (Grand Rapids, MI: Zondervan Publishing House, 1982), p.51 where it was referenced to Tim LaHaye, *How to Win Over Depression* (Grand Rapids, MI: Zondervan, 1974), p.89.
15. Jennifer Minney, *Beyond Depression* (Yeovil: Silvertree Publishing, 2001), p.27.

CHAPTER 3

1. Candace Pert, *Molecule of Emotion* (New York: Pocket Books, 1999), p.306.
2. Eugene H. Peterson, *The Message Remix* (Colorado Springs: NavPress, 2003), p.82.
3. Christine Ledger, *Shattered Dreams, A Mother's Pain* (Gloucester: Word for Life Trust, 2001), p.124.
4. Wendy Bray, *In the Palm of God's Hand* (Third Edition) (Oxford: Bible

Reading Fellowship, 2007).

5. Max Sinclair with Carolyn Armitage, *Halfway to Heaven* (London: Hodder & Stoughton, 1982). Used with permission.

CHAPTER 4

1. David W. Augsberger, *The Freedom of Forgiveness* (Chicago: Moody Press, 1970), pp.20-21.

2. Jay E. Adams, *The Christian Counsellor's Manual* (Nutley, NJ: Presbyterian and Reformed, 1973), pp.64-70.

3. Jay E. Adams, *How to Overcome Evil* (Grand Rapids, MI: Baker Book House, 1977), pp.89-90.

4. Names have been changed to protect the privacy of the family concerned.

5. For a practical and inspirational study of forgiveness in greater depth, we would recommend Johann Christoph Arnold's *The Lost Art of Forgiving* (Crowborough, Sussex: Plough, 1998).

National Distributors

UK: (and countries not listed below)
CWR, Waverley Abbey House, Waverley Lane, Farnham, Surrey GU9 8EP.
Tel: (01252) 784700 Outside UK (+44) 1252 784700

AUSTRALIA: CMC Australasia, PO Box 519, Belmont, Victoria 3216.
Tel: (03) 5241 3288 Fax: (03) 5241 3290

CANADA: Cook Communications Ministries, PO Box 98, 55 Woodslee Avenue, Paris, Ontario N3L 3E5.
Tel: 1800 263 2664

GHANA: Challenge Enterprises of Ghana, PO Box 5723, Accra.
Tel: (021) 222437/223249 Fax: (021) 226227

HONG KONG: Cross Communications Ltd, 1/F, 562A Nathan Road, Kowloon.
Tel: 2780 1188 Fax: 2770 6229

INDIA: Crystal Communications, 10-3-18/4/1, East Marredpalli, Secunderabad – 500026,
Andhra Pradesh.
Tel/Fax: (040) 27737145

KENYA: Keswick Books and Gifts Ltd, PO Box 10242, Nairobi.
Tel: (02) 331692/226047 Fax: (02) 728557

MALAYSIA: Salvation Book Centre (M) Sdn Bhd, 23 Jalan SS 2/64, 47300 Petaling Jaya, Selangor.
Tel: (03) 78766411/78766797 Fax: (03) 78757066/78756360

NEW ZEALAND: CMC Australasia, PO Box 303298, North Harbour, Auckland 0751.
Tel: 0800 449 408 Fax: 0800 449 049

NIGERIA: FBFM, Helen Baugh House, 96 St Finbarr's College Road, Akoka, Lagos.
Tel: (01) 7747429/4700218/825775/827264

PHILIPPINES: OMF Literature Inc, 776 Boni Avenue, Mandaluyong City.
Tel: (02) 531 2183 Fax: (02) 531 1960

SOUTH AFRICA: Struik Christian Books, 80 MacKenzie Street, PO Box 1144, Cape Town 8000.
Tel: (021) 462 4360 Fax: (021) 461 3612

SRI LANKA: Christombu Publications (Pvt) Ltd., Bartleet House, 65 Braybrooke Place,
Colombo 2. Tel: (9411) 2421073/2447665

TANZANIA: CLC Christian Book Centre, PO Box 1384, Mkwepu Street, Dar es Salaam.
Tel/Fax: (022) 2119439

USA: Cook Communications Ministries, PO Box 98, 55 Woodslee Avenue, Paris, Ontario N3L 3E5, Canada.
Tel: 1800 263 2664

ZIMBABWE: Word of Life Books (Pvt) Ltd, Christian Media Centre, 8 Aberdeen Road, Avondale,
PO Box A480 Avondale, Harare.
Tel: (04) 333355 or 091301188

For email addresses, visit the CWR website: www.cwr.org.uk

CWR is a registered charity – Number 294387

CWR is a limited company registered in England – Registration Number 1990308

Waverley Abbey Insight Series: Insight into Anxiety

What is anxiety? Who is at risk of it? How does anxiety affect us? These and other questions are discussed in this helpful book, which also offers guidelines on building coping skills.

ISBN: 978-1-85345-436-3
£7.50 (plus p&p)

Other titles available in the Waverley Abbey Insight Series

Insight into Eating Disorders
Helena Wilkinson

An eating disorder is like an iceberg, with the visible tip of symptoms dwarfed by the pain below the surface. Helena Wilkinson, who herself suffered from anorexia as a teenager, examines this complex subject – and gives help in thawing out the iceberg.

ISBN-13: 978-1-85345-410-3
ISBN-10: 1-85345-410-9
£7.50 (plus p&p)

Insight into Self-Esteem
Chris Ledger and Wendy Bray

An honest and personal approach to the problems of low self-esteem. Cultivating healthy self-esteem grows from a deepening relationship with God. The insights shared here incorporate a foundation of established research and a wealth of practical experience.

ISBN-13: 978-1-85345-409-7
ISBN-10: 1-85345-409-5
£7.50 (plus p&p)

Insight into Bereavement
Wendy Bray and
Diana Priest

Bereavements follow a similar path of loss, disbelief, grief and adaptation. This book provides sound advice on coping, whether the bereavement is of a loved one, a marriage or a livelihood. It looks at the effects of loss and at being a channel of God's love to the bereaved.

ISBN-13: 978-1-85345-385-4
ISBN-10: 1-85345-385-4
£7.50 (plus p&p)

Insight into Stress
Beverley Shepherd

An examination of the basics of stress, this book provides practical help and advice on this complex subject. Topics covered include how stress arises, recognising warning signs and coping with the demands and expectations of ourselves and others.

ISBN-13: 978-1-85345-384-7
ISBN-10: 1-85345-384-6
£7.50 (plus p&p)

Prices correct at time of printing